barcode in 2 pgs.

THE HIGH-TECH BICYCLE

EDWARD P. STEVENSON

Photographed by David Arky
Designed by Deborah Bracken

1817

HARPER & ROW, PUBLISHERS, New York

Cambridge, Philadelphia, San Francisco, London

Mexico City, São Paulo, Sydney

Published by Harper & Row, Publishers, Inc., 10 East 53rd Street, New York, N.Y. 10022

Library of Congress Cataloging in Publication Data

Stevenson, Edward P.
  High tech bicycle.

  Bibliography: p.
  Includes index.
  1. Bicycles.   I. Title.
TL410.S83   1982   629.2′272   81-48157
ISBN 0-06-014876-4   AACR2

82 83 84 85 86 10 9 8 7 6 5 4 3 2 1

Produced by The Jeffrey Weiss Group, Inc.,
133 Fifth Avenue, New York, N.Y. 10003

Illustrated by Alphonse Tvaryanas

ACKNOWLEDGMENTS

My sincere and heartfelt thanks to the proprietors of three of New York City's finest bicycle shops for their generous help and cooperation: Philip Williams of Bikes and Things, Gaylen Preheim of Toga Bike Shop, and Sarah and Conrad Weiss of Conrad's Bike Shop—and to their dedicated and knowledgeable staffs.

Additional thanks to Deborah Bracken for editorial advice and moral support above and beyond the call.

CREDITS

Additional photographs and illustrations:

Leonardo da Vinci bicycle, page 11, courtesy S. C. Williams Library, Stevens Institute of Technology, Hoboken, New Jersey.

Reproductions, pages 19, 20, 21, from *The Wheelman*, 1884, courtesy of the Jersey City Public Library, Jersey City, New Jersey.

Photo, page 80, courtesy of Shimano American Corporation, Parsippany, New Jersey.

Photos, page 153 and back cover, illustration, page 188, courtesy of Early Winters, Limited, Seattle, Washington.

Photo, page 156, courtesy of the Klein Corporation, Chehalis, Washington.

Photos, pages 157 (top and bottom), 175, 187, Yiorgos Naoum, Arcadia, California.

Photos, pages 183, 184, courtesy of Mechano-Physics Corporation, Honolulu, Hawaii.

Photo, page 190, courtesy of Zzip Designs, Bonny Doon California.

Photos, page 191, courtesy of Veltec, Boulder, Colorado

CONTENTS

This book is intended to be a number of things. On the broadest level, it is a celebration of fine bicycles—of their spare and simple beauty and of the craft and ingenuity that go into making them. More specifically, it is an attempt to increase understanding of what a fine bicycle is, what goes into its creation, how it works, and how it got to be that way. It is an attempt to provide an overview of the state of the art of bicycle building today and the technology that underlies it: a drawing together of many diverse threads of theory and practice. It is a report on the state of bicycling activities in America. Finally, it is a look at the experimental development efforts that promise to bring us radically different muscle-powered vehicles in the not-too-distant future.

INTRODUCTION

Much of what we are familiar with in the design of bicycles has been on the scene for close to a hundred years—an odd thought, perhaps, with which to begin a book on "high technology," but true nonetheless. The "safety" bicycle of the 1890s, mere technological adolescent that it was, was in most basic respects the same machine we know today. During the period that brought the "safety" into being, the concept of the bicycle underwent many profound and radical changes in design and technology; but, following its ascendancy, that evolutionary process slowed dramatically—the force of experimental energy was largely spent.

After the turn of the century change became slow and incremental and the primary component was in the direction of standardization. Nevertheless, the end product, the modern bicycle, is a fascinatingly sophisticated creation. Much of the thinking that has ultimately been put into practice in its design is characterized above all by its simplicity, or perhaps a better word is *refinement.*

Technological innovation often appears clumsy and complex when it is young, but the relentless scrutiny of people striving for something better is a powerful force. Successful technology—*mature* technology, we might call it—has invariably been through a lengthy process of refinement. I am fascinated by bicycles and their tantalizing mixture of sophistication and simplicity. It has taken time for the right ideas to be generated, thought through, and combined in ways that make bicycles do their simple thing better and better.

Today the situation is less static than at any time over the last fifty years. The pace of bicycle evolution has accelerated over the last decade-and-a-half. Bicycles are serious business in the 1980s and things are happening. As an abstract idea, the bicycle is still a mixture of refined design and young, experimental thinking; I find *both* facets engaging.

One of the factors that intrigues me is that the broad front of change embraces so many diverse paths and approaches, points of view and fields of endeavor. Some builders and experimenters in the bicycle world are devoting their energies to wringing that one last quantum of improvement from concepts, designs, and materials that are tried and true; others are searching for entirely new concepts, designs, and materials. Some thread a path between these extremes.

Making subtle but significant changes in the configuration of conventional frame design is an innovation that has brought fame to a number of Italian frame-builders in recent years. An innovation of an entirely different order has been the creation of a new steel alloy, which has allowed the building of lighter frames regardless of the tube angles. Going farther in the same direction has been the search for new materials with structural properties superior to that of steel. Several builders have made real pioneering efforts in the creation of bicycles in a completely new shape in order to utilize more effectively the inherent capacities of the human physique. "External" developments take such forms as the invention of fairings—even clothing—that make a bicycle easier to ride, regardless of its shape; or the development of an electronic device that allows the rider to keep more closely in touch with the physiological effects of training.

Old forms are being rethought and ways are being found to improve on almost every traditional form in bicycle building—forms that have been accepted uncritically for decades. Some of these changes are minute and marginal in their effects; some are sizable, suggesting sweeping changes in the whole shape and appearance of bicycles. To me it is a source of wonder to see the diversity of inputs all directed toward the same aim—making cycles (not all cycles will be *bi-* in the world to come) work better.

Why the big upswing in bicycle development? Simple: People have become interested in using bicycles. Over the past ten to fifteen years a significant portion of the population, numbering in the millions, has been discovering (or rediscovering) the joys of cycling—creating a new climate of excitement and change. Industry statistics show a doubling of bicycle sales over the past decade and a fourfold increase in bicycle use over the past two—an unexpected development for our petroleum-guzzling nation.

During this period, however, there have been other unexpected developments and our world has undergone some shocking, traumatic changes, resulting in a vastly different set of economic expectations for too many of us. As we turn our ingenuity to the problem of coexisting successfully with our new universe—consuming less, being more rational and more efficient, marshaling our resources more intelligently and disturbing the other inhabitants of our world less—the bicycle seems in many ways a perfect companion.

It doesn't consume. It doesn't pollute. It does confer significant health benefits on its users. After a comparatively small initial investment, it provides a virtually cost-free means of transportation for both practical and recreational purposes that operates efficiently within the range that most people move in their daily lives.

For some riders the bicycle is no more than a tool, a method of travel; but for most, I think, it is an important instrument of enjoyment, of recreation either casual or serious— often intensely serious.

Competitive racing is as old as anything that could be called a bicycle, despite the fact that the present-day American public hasn't had much contact with the sport. Bike racing, by and large, is not reported on the sports pages of our newspapers. TV coverage of the Olympic Games ignores it almost completely. Nevertheless, dormant for more than forty years, the sport has taken a new lease on life, and American competitors are beginning to hold their own with the best riders from nations where cycling has been more or less the undisputed king of sports for the better part of a century.

Bicycle racing at its most competitive is a grueling sport and not everyone's cup of tea. For the less ambitious who would nevertheless like to test their skill and prowess on a lesser scale, racing opportunities exist all across the country for riders of all ages and levels of ability. It doesn't matter that there are rarely large crowds of cheering fans; cycling is first and foremost a participatory sport. There are very few bike-racing fans who are not also involved in cycling in some way—as opposed to almost all the other sports that we follow. That exhilaration, the peak experience that comes from giving something your best effort, is available to all.

Cycle touring is also essentially a participatory activity. Obviously there is little chance of anyone's enjoying cycle touring sitting in a grandstand or in front of a TV set. Rather, as a mode of travel, it involves interaction with the environment—contact with the land and weather. As a cycle tourist, you touch the earth regardless of whether you spend your nights at home, in hotels or hostels, or under the open sky. Your vision and your hearing are unobstructed. You get the scents and the sounds—and you feel the bumps, too. You *experience* the country you are traveling through.

By comparison, driving through the countryside in a car is much more like seeing a movie. The road guides your perception of the surroundings, especially if you are the driver. It is usually difficult to stop; and, unless you are deliberately taking a scenic, backroads route (which few people do), chances are you will pass by a great deal of beauty too quickly to comprehend it.

So bicycle touring offers a sense of participation and contact with the world; and, very often, having made a long, perhaps arduous, journey entirely under your own power leads to a kind of peak experience as well. At the very least, it should instill a feeling of self-confidence and independence. I, for one, think that these are experiences and feelings that we are going to need more and more in the years to come as other aspects of our lives become more regimented, more controlled by mechanization—which is what the future seems to hold for us.

I have been using a number of emotional terms here—peak experience, feelings of participation, self-confidence—and for a reason. I think there is a strong emotional component in most people's relationships to bicycles and bicycling, and I think this derives in large part from the very simplicity and straightforwardness of bicycles that I alluded to earlier.

The mystique that surrounds so many of the machines that surround us—that are, we are told, too complex for us to understand—produces a subtle feeling of alienation in most of us, a sense of helplessness or, in other words, dependency. There is no mystery with the bicycle. It's all right there in plain view—well, practically. Anyone who has the desire can, with a minimal investment in tools and information, do all the maintenance and repair that the bicycle will ever need. That helps one to feel *in control*—an increasingly rare experience. It is being self-sufficient rather than dependent and it's good for us psychically.

Finally, as if all the foregoing wasn't enough, cycling is good for us physically as well. The recent "craze" for cardiovascular fitness that followed on the heels of our not-so-recent period of involvement with inner-psychic consciousness (largely revealed through the use of drugs), has propelled cycling into the limelight along with jogging, swimming, and a few other athletic pursuits. Even making allowances for my personal preference, I suspect that cycling will eventually be seen as the most attractive alternative of the currently popular general conditioning sports. The reason is simple: Cycling is more fun (less boring) and much less physically punishing than the rest.

Any nation that can put men on the moon ought to be able to devise a human-powered vehicle capable of breaking the national highway speed limit of 55 miles per hour, or so reasoned Dr. Allan Abbott, experimental cycle designer and holder of the world's record for motor-paced cycle speed. In 1976 Dr. Abbott established a prize for the first unassisted vehicle, powered by one or more human "engines," to top the 55 mile-an-hour pace over a 200-meter course. Today, that goal has already been achieved—the barrier broken, the prize collected.

As we pass the milestone of the beginning of the '80s we have access to bicycles that surpass the wildest hopes of the past. At the same time, we stand on the threshold of future developments that we can only guess at the shape of now. Historical accident, the vicissitudes of human affairs, and the coming together of a vast array of technological achievements and breakthroughs combine to create a situation in which fairly massive resources are likely to be devoted to making not just significant but radical alterations and improvements in what we are accustomed to thinking of as the bicycle. These future "human-powered vehicles" may go a long way toward replacing the vehicles that now threaten to bankrupt us with their thirst for a dwindling supply of petroleum. For me there is a special poetic satisfaction in that scenario. It reminds me of another trend of the '80s: the replacement of air conditioning and electric lighting with —windows.

The idea of a human-powered or "manumotive" vehicle based on nature's miracle, the wheel, was one that floated to the surface of Western culture from time to time over many centuries. The remarkable Leonardo da Vinci made sketches of a bicyclelike device more than 300 years before we know of any such machine being built. For Leonardo, like many others, the idea had *begun* to take shape, but it remained only an idea. It took the general awakening of the European mechanical mind—the impetus of that ferocious outpouring of technological creativity that we now call the industrial revolution—to turn that dream into reality.

BACKGROUNDS

Curiously, considering the outcome, the muscle-driven cycle was not initially one of those products of man's inventive powers applied to *practical* problems. It had its beginnings as a product of human whimsy: It was a toy. Nevertheless, once its practical possibilities *were* comprehended, the designing and building of bicycles quickly became a serious business. The development of the bicycle was inextricably tied up in the development of mechanical and engineering technology in general; and conversely, its development spawned specific designs, materials, and techniques that

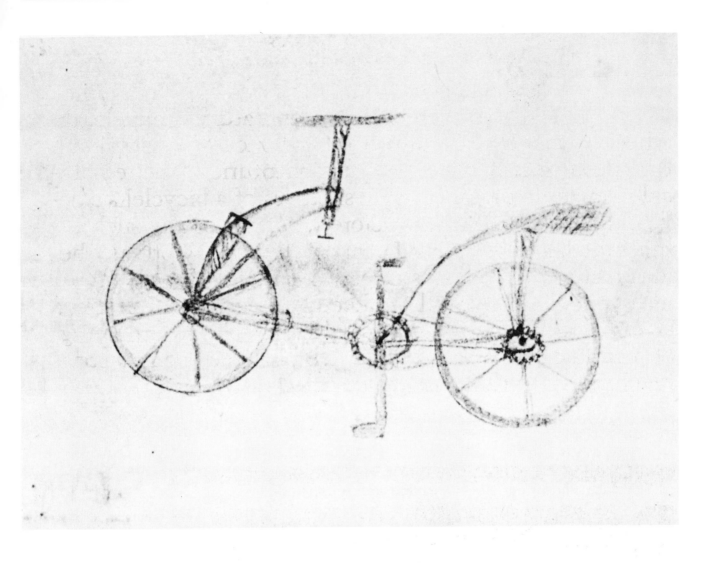

made possible further progress in a number of other areas—most notably the development of the automobile and the airplane.

Few people realize how rapid the development of the bicycle *was,* once it truly got under way. The first forerunner of the bicycle appeared before the turn of the last century. The first two-wheel, in-line vehicle with a mechanical propulsion system

This recently discovered drawing in the sketchbook known as the <u>Codex Atlanticus</u> (1503–4) is undoubtedly the brainchild of Leonardo da Vinci (although the drawing is probably not by his hand). It bears a remarkable resemblance to a mid-1880s safety bicycle.

that we know of was invented around 1840. The first true bicycle that succeeded in attracting general attention appeared in 1861, and this marked the beginning of the real whirlwind period of development. From then on the pace of change was incredibly rapid and the bicycle arrived at more or less the form in which we know it today before the turn of this century. That is almost one-hundred years from the first physical manifestation of the concept; thirty years from the creation of the first "successful" rendition. Let's take a closer look at this remarkable history.

Scholars and historians disagree about the earliest appearances of depictions of objects that *might* have been precursors of the bicycle; but they *do* generally agree that it was a device named the "Célerifère" by its creator, one Monsieur de Sivrac, and "unleashed" by him in the gardens of the *Palais Royale* in Paris in 1791 that *did* lead more or less directly to the bicycle. The Célerifère consisted of two wheels mounted in line and connected by forks to a wooden bar, or "spine," on which was mounted a padded saddle. The rider straddled the spine in much the same way that we straddle a modern bike, but propulsion was provided by the feet pushing directly against the ground; the rider

ran along, pushing alternately with one foot and then the other. On smooth, level ground, this provided a significant mechanical advantage to the rider, but as the wheels were mounted rigidly in line it was difficult to travel in any but a straight line.

M. de Sivrac apparently dreamed up the Célerifère simply as a means of astonishing and terrifying the ladies that strolled in the public gardens—nothing more. However, as so often happens, the thing quickly got out of hand. The machine became an overnight fad among the fashionable young

The Draisienne or steerable hobby-horse. The raised platform behind the steering bar served to support the rider's chest as the vehicle was pushed along with the feet.

men of Paris, among whom it became known as the "Vélocifère." These aficionados dubbed *themselves* "Les Vélocipèdes," and organized races along the Champs Elysées. It was very likely in this context that someone first discovered, descending a hill, that a vehicle with two wheels in line could be balanced upright without the aid of the feet touching the ground. It was a significant discovery, but the Vélocifère itself remained a toy—the skateboard of its day—something on which the young and daring could perform astonishing feats, but little more.

The development that headed the hobbyhorse (as it had become known in England) in the direction of more practical applications is generally credited by historians to a German—Karl, Baron von Drais de Sauerbrun. Von Drais' improvement was a simple but significant one. By passing the front fork upward through the spine and attaching a steering bar, he made a new machine that could easily be guided anywhere the rider wanted to go. Although von Drais created his new version of the Vélocifère expressly for his own personal use on the estate on which he worked as agriculturist and "Master of the Woods and Forests," it created a sensation among his friends and acquaintances

who persuaded him to take it to Paris—which he did, in 1818. Paris received the improved Vélocifère (which quickly became known as the "Draisienne") with as much fervor as von Drais' friends, and so began a new chapter.

The popularity of the Draisienne spread across the channel to England where it revived the interest in hobbyhorses, which had been flagging somewhat. The able use of this vehicle became *de riguer* for young gentlemen, both French and English. Schools sprang up to teach the timid to master this unpredictable two-legged beast, and the satirists in the press of both countries had a field day.

But while the hobbyhorse, albeit improved, remained primarily a plaything of the leisure classes, it began immediately to attract more serious attention as a potential means of transportation. After all it was possible, under favorable conditions, to travel upwards of fifty miles in a day with its aid—certainly more than an unaided walker could manage. The Draisienne's potential or utility remained firmly in the minds of a number of children of their age—firm believers in the notion that in machines lay the future, the salvation, and the prosperity of mankind. A long series of attempts was made to trans-

form it into something newer still: a vehicle that could be propelled independently of body contact with the ground.

The principles of mechanics were becoming ever more widely understood during these years, and new principles were being discovered and new solutions to problems perfected constantly. A number of inventors, including some who were responsible for highly significant achievements in the design of industrial machinery, worked on solutions to the problem of mechanical propulsion of wheeled vehicles over the next couple of decades; but most of the solutions proved too complex to be of practical use and were abandoned.

What should certainly have been another major turning point in our story was the year 1840 (some say 1839), in which a Scottish blacksmith, Kirkpatrick Macmillan, invented and built the first known pedal-driven (or, more correctly, treadle-driven) cycle. The mechanism was admirably simple (as are so many of the best inventions). The base of Macmillan's bicycle was a fairly ordinary Draisienne with a rear wheel somewhat larger than the front and with the addition of crank arms fixed to the hub of the rear wheel. The ends of the cranks were attached to long rods that ran forward and were in turn connected to

The first known mechanically propelled bicycle, built by Kirkpatrick Macmillan around 1840. Its system of rods and treadles, used to drive the cranks on the rear wheel, was employed on a few later bicycles, but never really caught on.

vertical rods at the front of the cycle that swung, pendulum-fashion, as the longitudinal rods moved back and forth. A wooden platform was attached to the end of each of the vertical rods to accommodate the rider's foot. Once the machine was in forward motion (which was probably accomplished hobbyhorse-style), the rider maintained locomotion by pushing the treadles alternately. The main skill required to operate the cycle was the ability to coordinate the pushing of the treadle—basically a vertical motion—with the rotation of the rear wheel. Anyone who has operated a premotorized sewing machine will understand.

Macmillan's bicycle was apparently quite effi-cient—he rode it on the roads of his native Dumfriesshire to the end of his days—but, although it was copied by others who came into contact with Macmillan, the design died out without ever gaining general notice or acceptance. It was simply an evolutionary dead end—a species that appeared in an environment that failed to provide enough nurture. Less metaphorically it was a case of an invention coming along too early in the history of communications and in too isolated an area for the idea to spread. Had Macmillan lived in London (or had he taken his bicycle there), the wave of interest, activity, and ingenuity that was ultimately spawned by the bicycle might have been

generated twenty years earlier than it was.

So Fortune's Wheel was destined to make a few more revolutions before another individual was to receive the inspiration necessary to make a successful bicycle. In 1861 Pierre Michaux, a Parisian pram maker, had the idea of attaching crank arms to the hub of a Draisienne he was repairing—this time to the front wheel. Michaux's inspiration was in associating the wheel he was gazing at with a crank-driven grindstone. He attached pedals to the ends of the crank arms, just like a present-day child's tricycle, and lo! the Vélocipède was born. The whole problem of a mechanical linkage between the driving parts of the body

The Michaux veloc-
ipede: the bicycle
that finally "made it."

and the wheel of the cycle had been eliminated; the only problem remaining was to position the rider's body so that his or her feet could reach the pedals. This Michaux accomplished quickly as he set about to produce a viable prototype of his invention.

Paris, unlike rural Scotland twenty years earlier, turned out to be a favorable environment for the new invention, one in which it was destined to prosper. Michaux, being an astute and aggressive businessman, took full advantage of his position in what its inhabitants considered the

capital of world culture and devoted his considerable energies to improving, manufacturing, promoting, and selling his machines. Hundreds were built by the firm in the next few years, and considerable refinements of design and manufacture were achieved. Demand far outstripped supply, and soon there were competing Parisian manufacturers vying for a piece of the trade. It was not long before the seeds of competition were sown across the channel as well.

In 1867 a young Englishman, Rowley Turner,

Paris agent for the Coventry Sewing Machine Co., was showing his firm's wares at the Paris Exposition of that year, at which Michaux's velocipedes were also being exhibited. Turner caught the bug immediately, and the following year he brought a Michaux machine back to Coventry and persuaded his firm to go into bicycle production. Reorganized in 1869 into the Coventry Machinists Company, Ltd., this firm provided the initial spark for the British cycle-building industry and served as the cradle for much of the inventive and engineering talent that contributed to its ascendancy over the next three decades. Turner himself was very much a prototype of the sort of person who has been associated with cycling throughout its history: He fell in love with the machine and its possibilities and thereafter devoted all of his energies to developing and promoting cycling.

The velocipede (or "boneshaker" as the British called it) arose from the technology of the carriage-building trade and, in the beginning was based on the same materials and techniques— wood and iron, joined and forged in traditional ways. The typical, "classic" velocipede of circa 1868 had a driving wheel of about 36 inches in diameter and a rear wheel of about 30 inches. The rigid spokes were either wooden or iron rods. Wheel hubs were wood or iron, depending on the composition of the spokes. Axles and bearings were either of iron or, in some instances, of machined brass. Rims were generally wooden, sometimes shod with iron. Cranks were affixed directly to the front-wheel axle. Pedals took a number of forms.

The "backbone" of the boneshaker, which constituted most of the frame as we would now think of it, was a

sloping, or sometimes a gently S-curving, member, usually of iron. At its front end it held the steering tube. From there it swept backward to the point at which it divided

into a fork to accommodate the rear wheel. The front fork came together in a steering column that passed up through the backbone, ending in a straight steering bar. The

saddle was attached to a suspended leaf spring, which was supported on a fork from the rear wheel and which was attached to the backbone in a variety of ways. Total weight was in the vicinity of 50 to 60 pounds.

This, then, was the machine that set the ball rolling, as it were. What was it capable of in performance terms? Well, since there was really nothing previous to compare it to (aside from horse-drawn carriages), few if any "objective" performance data were kept for the early velocipedes. People were too busy discovering the joy and excitement of riding to focus on statistics.

One statement we can make with certainty is that it was undeniably capable of arousing the human competitive instinct. Informal racing sprang up instantly. (That tradition went back to the days of the Vélocifère.) It was as much a way of comparing machines as of comparing personal prowess. By 1868, however, "official" racing appeared on the scene. In June of that year the first recorded "official" race was held at Saint-Cloud, near Paris. It was a 1,200-meter event held on a specially built track. The winner was an Englishman, James Moore. (The first recorded British race was held on the very next day, at Hendon.) The following year saw

the first long-distance race—approximately 83 miles from Paris to Rouen. Moore was again the winner in a time of just under 10½ hours, and his fellow countryman and enthusiast Rowley Turner also placed high among the finishers, earning a medal.

The almost-instant craze of bicycle racing was certainly one of the pressures—perhaps the most important one—that motivated bicycle builders to improve their products—and improve they did, almost from the first moment. Speed was the objective, and there were several obvious routes to that objective: making the machine lighter; improving the efficiency of its moving parts; and, most important, increasing the drive capacity—making the cycle travel farther for each revolution of the cranks. While all these problems were being worked on simultaneously, it was the solutions to the third that had the most impact on the appearance, the physical form of the bicycle, for the next fifteen years.

In the absence of some form of gearing, the only way to get the cycle to go faster—to travel farther for every turn of the pedals—was to increase the diameter of the driving wheel. (It must be pointed out that gearing systems were invented early on, but the imagination of builder

and riding public alike seems to have been drawn to the other idea—making the driving wheel bigger.) The classic Michaux velocipede, as mentioned, had a driving wheel of about 36 inches in diameter and a rear wheel of about 30 inches. As early as 1869 boneshakers were being built with front wheels twice as large as the trailing wheel. Over the succeeding five years there was a constant trend in the direction of ever-bigger driving wheels and, by the middle of the 1870s, standard models, called "ordinaries," had front wheels of between 42 and 60 inches in diameter. In some of the more extreme versions, the rear trailing wheel was as small as one third the diameter of the driving wheel—or *less*.

Typical models at the beginning of the decade had 48-inch driving wheels and 24-inch trailing wheels. Just this amount of wheel-size increase would have been unwieldy if there hadn't been ancillary developments in wheel-building technology. The year 1869 saw the first "suspended" bicycle wheel—one that used light, ductile spokes rather than rigid ones. Two years later designs emerged in which spoke tension was made adjustable. One of these was the work of James Starley (of the Coventry Machinists). The wheels of Starley's "Ariel" bicycle

James Starley's 'Ariel'—the first bicycle to use a "suspended" wheel with tensioned spokes.

had a lever fastened to the hub spindle and, by means of tie rods connecting the ends of this lever to the rim, the overall tension of the wheel could be adjusted. The "Tension" bicycle, introduced in the same year as the Ariel, used threaded nipples to adjust the tension of each spoke individually—the system still employed today. W.H.J. Grout is the English designer credited with this invention. Some of the other improvements first exhibited on these

beginning-of-the-decade machines were round, hollow rubber tires (not pneumatic yet); hollow forks, raked and sprung for improved handling and comfort; and a 2:1 "speed gear."

As the 1870s sped by other technological innovations and improvements emerged. Among the more significant were wheel hubs with forged-steel spindles mounted in adjustable ball bearings; lightweight, hollow-section frame members; and

strong steel wheel rims. As this was going on the shape of the bicycle continued to develop in the direction of larger and larger front driving wheels and smaller and smaller rear trailing wheels.

Ordinaries (also known as "high-wheelers" in the U.S. and "penny-farthings" in England—an apparent allusion to the image of the large English penny next to the diminutive farthing) were built throughout the '70s *and* the following decade. During this time the size of the driving wheels gradually climbed into the 60-inch range and beyond, as every conceivable variation on the basic idea was explored. But while ordinaries captured most of the attention, they were not the only game in town. As a matter of fact, in its extremity, the design of the ordinary carried the seeds of its own destruction. There were serious probs- associated with it.

First of all, on the simplest level, they were hard to

A typical "ordinary" bicycle. One of the first problems in riding an ordinary was getting on.

mount—increasingly so as they grew in size. With the large racing high-wheelers the rider literally required an assistant to get onto his machine and start the race. Second, they favored certain types of physiques almost to the exclusion of other people. The ordinary was built with the large and long-legged male rider in mind; all others were at a disadvantage. Finally, and most important, was that they were extremely dangerous to ride, especially on the public roads. In order to position the rider for maximum efficiency in pedaling, designers tended to place the saddle so that most of the rider's weight was centered over the driving wheel. In any case in which a sudden stop or upset occurred—any stone or pothole in the road—the rider was likely to take a header over the handlebars and end up in a hospital or a pine box. Serious injuries were frequent.

Now it is true that for some the danger and hardship of cycle riding was part of the excitement, but while those adventurous cyclists gladly opted for the high-spirited high-wheeler, there was a quiet movement afoot to create a bicycle that was less hazardous to ride and was more suited to use by people of smaller stature.

Just as an attempt to clarify the next part of the discussion, it must be pointed out that, like the origin of the species, the evolution of the modern bicycle was a gradual and rather convoluted process, *not* proceeding in a linear fashion. In fact during this

period (roughly 1875 to 1890) there were several overlapping evolutions going on simultaneously. There was the first progression from the boneshaker to the high-wheeler and the attempts to perfect the latter—make it lighter, faster, more efficient—which went on well into the '90s. Then, because of the problems encountered with the high-wheel bicycle, there was a sort of reverse evolution, backward from the classic giants, that attempted to preserve their principal characteristics while modifying the design to make them safer and accessible to a broader group of riders. Finally, there were designers who were exploring radically new concepts that didn't draw at all on the thinking that created the ordinary. Enterprising designers who were also astute businessmen realized that potential markets for their machines were much greater, especially if they could design bicycles that were faster *and* safer.

It was in the second half of the 1870s that the term "safety bicycle" began to be heard. Again, the first "safety" designs were generally attempts to make the ordinary more stable. Initial modifications involved compromising the size of the driving wheel somewhat, down to the 48- to 50-inch range, and throwing the center of gravity definitely backward. This, along with an increase in the size and weight of the trailing wheel and an increase in tire width, did achieve a considerable improvement in stability—at a significant reduction in performance.

These 'Pioneer' bicycles were among the early attempts to make ordinaries safer by moderating their extreme dimensions. Note the lever-linked crank-and-pedal system.

One such early "safety," the Singer Xtra-Ordinary Challenge, used pivoted linkage rods to connect the pedals to the crank arms, as the new position of the rider made it impossible for the legs to reach the conventional pedal axis. Designed by George Singer (who, like Starley, had been former foreman at Coventry Machinists), this bicycle was in all respects a high-tech machine. Its 50-inch driving wheel was built around forged steel axles mounted in double, adjustable ball bearings within bronze, flanged hubs. The steering head was of a new (Starley) design with hardened steel "pivots" (not ball bearings yet). The forks were of hollow section and of aerodynamic design. The main frame member was made from hollow steel tubing. The whole machine was finely finished in black lacquer and nickel plate. Built for safety rather than performance it was nonetheless an adequate cycle for most purposes. Compared to the lightweight ordinaries, however, it was weighty indeed, tipping the scales at 54 pounds. (The refined high-wheeler was trimmed down to approximately 35 pounds during the '80s and special lightweight models were produced for racers, weighing in at as little as 22 pounds.)

A contemporary of the Singer Xtra was the "Facile," which was a bit smaller and substantially lighter (maximum front-wheel size, 48 inches; weight, 43 pounds). While the Facile was a very successful design, much of its commercial success was due to the efforts of its makers (Willis & Co., London) in pro-

The 'Star' bicycle—the "backwards" ordinary—an American solution to the safety problem. It was a very efficient bicycle, but it died out from the competition with more advanced designs.

motion of their product. They hit on the idea of sponsoring races for Faciles only (not unlike one-class sailing races today) and offered prizes for particular accomplishments and records to be established on their machines. Among the feats performed on the Facile by the intrepid (professional) rider J.H. Adams were the establishment of a 24-hour record of 221 ¼ miles, and the breaking of the Land's End—to— John o'Groat's record (that is a trek of approxi-

mately 800 miles from the southernmost point on the coast of Cornwall to the northern tip of Scotland)—accomplishing the journey in just under seven days.

Three years later, with the introduction of a new model Facile with "planetary" or epicyclic gearing that effectively increased wheel diameter by some 30 percent, records continued to fall. A rider from the Brixton Ramblers Bicycle Club collected the prize offered for being the

first to travel 300 miles within twenty-four hours. (Actually, he fell three miles short, but the prize was awarded anyway.) This record, an average of more than 12 miles per hour for a continuous twenty-four hours, is astonishing when you compare it to the single hour record of 14.3 miles posted by James Moore a decade before.

Another interesting attempt to diminish the hazards of the high-wheeler was

the American bicycle, the Star, manufactured under two different patents during the 1880s. The Star had a radically different look. It anticipated the later, true safety bicycle by making the rear wheel the driver (possibly the first to do so since Macmillan's 1840 machine). This gave a very bottom-heavy appearance to the machine, but dynamically the design was perfectly sound, and having the steering as well as the second, weight-balancing wheel in front of the driver eliminated the pitching-over problem entirely. The design of the Star was novel in other respects, too. Its propulsion system may well have been the only one ever put into production that did not utilize some sort of arrangement of cranks. Instead it used two levers, pivoted behind the real axle, which engaged ratcheted pawls on the rear hub. Pressing down either lever caused the hub to rotate forward. Upon release, the hub "freewheeled," much like a modern ratcheted hub. Springs returned the levers to the upright position. The standard method of "pedaling" the Star was, naturally, to alternate feet; but for an extra sprint or jump, both levers could be operated simultaneously. The Star achieved considerable success as a racing machine in this country for a time, but the design was never adopted outside the States. It was an evolutionary dead end.

While some designers, then, were working along the lines of developing ideas derived from the ordinary, others were exploring entirely new ideas and the term "safety bicycle," which had heralded the line of development we have just examined, began to take on new meaning. To reassert the analogy between human evolution and bicycle evolution, the set of ideas that eventually came together to produce the modern bicycle as we know it made its appearance long before it became dominant, just as Cro-Magnon man was getting a toehold in life during the same period in which the Neanderthals were in ascendancy.

As early as 1869 an English inventor named Shearing published a design for a rear-driven bicycle with a *chain* as its means of transmission. The idea never got beyond the concept stage,

however. Seven years later, another Englishman, George Shergold, actually built a very similar machine. The prototype is preserved, but again, it did not attract sufficient attention to be developed commercially.

Now gearing was the *sine qua non* of the "dwarf" or true safety bicycle. (The newly emerging breed was rather contemptuously dubbed "the dwarfs" by the industry for which the high-wheeler had become the norm.) It was the only reasonable means of reducing the driving wheel to manageable size and still having the machine go fast. One of the most significant features of the chain-drive concept, which makers were apparently slow to comprehend, was the beautiful simplicity it offered to the problem (or process, anyway) of gearing. Any conceivable, useful gear ratio could be achieved merely by selecting a suitable ratio of teeth between the chain wheel and the drive sprocket.

The first so-called dwarf safety bicycle that was actually put into commercial production—a rear-driven, chain-driven machine—was designed by H.J. Lawson, who is generally awarded the title "inventor of the safety bicycle" in encyclopedias, etc. Lawson's "Bicyclette," which made its first appearance at a trade show in 1880, had

wheels of unequal size (the driving wheel being smaller, oddly enough) and a rather cumbersome and complex steering system that used rod linkages to connect the handle-bars to the steering head. It achieved a measure of success with the public for whom constant change and innovation had become a fact of life. While Lawson did go on to design other models, he didn't really carry his ideas much further. The Lawson Bicyclette was close, but it wasn't yet "it."

The safety bicycle that finally made it was the third in a series of rear-, chain-driven Rover models—the work of James Starley's bright and experienced nephew John Kemp Starley. Rover I was a fairly typical dwarf ordinary with indirect steering. The next year's product added direct steering and brought the wheels closer to equality in size. The third model, which arrived on the scene in 1885, had equal-sized wheels and something very much like a modern, diamond frame.

Like the manufacturers of the Facile and other machines before him, J.K. Starley was astute enough to organize and promote races and competitions using his bicycles. In a 100-mile Rover race the previously existing record for the distance was broken by the winner, George Smith. Time: a bit over seven hours,

five minutes. A bicycle that was safe, relatively comfortable, *and* the fastest thing around simply *had* to succeed.

    The success of Starley's Rover did not end experimentation, of course. A number of other mechanical solutions to problems of frame geometry, suspension, transmission, and steering were tried. The so-called cross frame (resurrected in the early 1960s by the English cycle-designer Alexander Moulton) was one of the designs that appeared in the mid-1880s, was used with considerable success for a while, then abandoned. At least two distinct shaft-driven bicycles were built and marketed. These worked on a principle very much like a modern automobile transmission with pedaling torque being turned into longitudinal torque (a turning shaft running from the pedals to the rear wheel) and transformed once again into wheel torque. There was a bicycle, the "Whippet," that eased the bumps and potholes of the road by placing the points of contact, the handlebars, and saddle on a separate, sprung frame. The Whippet enjoyed considerable popularity for a while. But gradually all of the

John Kemp Starley's third 'Rover' bicycle, the first design that embodied most of the salient features of the modern bike: equal-sized wheels, chain drive to the rear wheel, a diamond frame, and direct steering.

ferment of experimentation began to die down. Certain designs came to be accepted as "the best." The Rover had many of these, but not all.

First, there was frame geometry. Many designers and manufacturers were getting close to the frame configuration that we think of as standard today; Starley's Rover was one. But the first bicycle with the precise arrangement of straight tubes—a main structure consisting of horizontal top tube, a slanting head tube more or less parallel to the seat tube and joined to it by a downward sloping "down" tube; front fork joined in a steering tube that ran inside the head tube; rear triangle formed by "stays" that supported the rear wheel—is generally credited to the firm of Humber where it was perfected in the late '80s. Again, while other frame designs were tried after the appearance of the now-familiar "diamond," they all ultimately withered away and were abandoned.

Perhaps the most significant development for cycling, once the safety bicycle had arrived at its more or less static form, was the creation of the pneumatic tire—the invention of John Boyd Dunlop, a Belfast veterinarian who liked to tinker. Dunlop created the first crude pneumatic tires for his son's bicycle, so the story goes, but this was

not an invention to fall by the wayside. After perfecting the product, Dunlop took out a patent on his invention in 1888. Almost immediately a company was formed to manufacture the 2-inch diameter inflated tires. Although they were quite costly in comparison to the solid or hollow (but unpressurized) rubber tires commonly in use at the time, they gained popularity rapidly.

Dunlop's pneumatic tires were contemptuously dubbed "sausages" by the rugged pros who still stuck to the ordinary and its technology; but, once again, it was a race result that turned the tide of sentiment and history. In the first recorded race in which the new pneumatic tires were used (in 1889), a rider from the Belfast Cruisers Cycle Club beat a strong field of competitors on ordinaries; the "big men" had, in effect, to eat their ridicule of the "sausage." Within a few years pneumatic tires had virtually replaced the older solids. After all it was another of those improvements that carried a double punch. It provided significantly improved comfort and safety for the rider *and* made the bicycle go faster.

It was the principle of gearing that allowed the size of the driving wheel to be brought down to the point at which other aspects of bicycle

design could receive due consideration. Not content with this, however, several inventors, designers, and engineers began working out systems of *variable* gearing, starting in the 1880s. Several multiple-ratio gearing systems were patented and put into use before the turn of the century; but it was the internal, rear-hub, three-speed gearing system invented by Henry Sturmey and James Archer that became the most widely used. Sturmey and Archer took their epicyclic or planetary gearing system to the then-young Raleigh firm who agreed to manufacture it. Raleigh, first entering the bicycle business in 1888, had from the beginning made variable gears one of their selling points. They recognized a superior product in Sturmey and Archer's invention and the new gear hub, patented by the inventors in 1902, quickly became standard equipment on Raleigh bicycles. The Sturmey-Archer three-speed hub was not the first variable gearing system to be invented or to be put into use, but it was the simplest—which made it easier and cheaper to manufacture. In addition it had one feature that was new: freewheel capacity in all gears. It was a relatively recent idea, the freewheel. Up until the late '80s no one had questioned the idea that, if you were going downhill, you put your feet on the footrest provided by the manufacturer for that purpose and let the cranks spin. The ability to coast at will, keeping the feet on the pedals, was a big improvement in convenience *and* safety. By combining variable gearing with a freewheeling hub, Sturmey and Archer created an eminently salable product and dealt yet another double blow to the primitive beginnings of cycling.

One final development that took place before the turn of the century, affecting the performance but not the appearance of bicycles, was the establishment of the Patented Butted Tube Company in 1898 by A.M. Reynolds. Reynolds had been working for years trying to perfect lightweight bicycle tubing when, in 1887, he invented the tube-forming process he called "butting"—making the tube sections thicker at the ends where stress was concentrated in use and thinner in the middle so the tube could be as light as possible. The butting process effectively optimized the ratio of strength to weight in steel bicycle tubing. Although the composition of the steels used in cycle tubing has changed over the past eighty years, the process of forming it has not. Reynolds' process is still very much in use (and the Butted Tube Company,

The Dursley-Pedersen (ca. 1894) was the Rolls-Royce of its day. It combined a carefully engineered, fully triangulated frame design with the finest materials and impeccable workmanship.

now known as TI Reynolds is still alive and well).

With all the improvements and innovations incorporated, the wild beast in the early bicycle had been truly tamed. The final decade of the nineteenth century and the first decade of the twentieth were without a doubt the period of the most immoderate adoration of bicycles and bicycling that the world has ever experienced. *Everyone* rode a bicycle—from the working classes to royalty, men and women alike. The cycles of the wealthy were painted and decorated to match the dressing habits of their owners. Bicycling permeated popular culture to a degree that few realize today, working its way into novels, plays, and dozens of popular songs. During the same period it became the backbone of postal and other delivery systems and was first honed as a tool of warfare.

Although innovation did not cease, the bicycle

trade in general settled down from a course of fearless, freewheeling experimentation to one of gradual, steady refinement and, in some cases, "gentrification." Both the pressures of capitalization and the reality of governmental and industrial standards for the huge fleets of machines now being used in work life pushed the cycle trade in the direction of larger, more efficient manufacturing organizations and the standardization of many parts and components.

As a focal point of technological development the bicycle was discarded in favor of the newly emerging motor-powered vehicles: motorcycles, automobiles, and airplanes. Those and a World War helped to distract the attention of the public from the cherished bicycle. But, although eclipsed, the bicycle continued to prosper quietly in the shadows, emerging once again in the 1970s as an object worthy of passion.

Although (ironically) the organized sport of bicycle racing has tended to impose an over-all conservative influence on the acceptance of innovation, much of the impetus for improvement and technological development in bicycle building has come from racers.

CYCLE RACING

Bicycle racing—serious bicycle racing—takes a lot of guts. It is a grueling, punishing sport. It may not be the single most taxing athletic activity (cross-country ski racing seems to have that distinction), but it does test men's and women's capacities way down deep. Bodily strength and stamina, will power, skill in bike handling, a knowledge of strategy, an instinct for tactics, the ability to make split-second assessments—of one's own capacities as well as those of one's opponents—and act on them, courage, the capacity to withstand pain, the ability to reach down inside oneself and find that extra quantum of energy at the right moment—all of these and more go into winning bicycle races.

Bicycle racing can be baffling, too, to those who are not familiar with its rituals and realities. Watching two riders moving slowly, apparently aimlessly, up and down the sides of a steeply banked oval track, like four-year-olds on tricycles, suddenly transformed into churning, flying projectiles for a few moments of dazzling speed; watching a mass of silent, concentrated, perspiring riders circle a half-mile track for hours on end in a curious, ever-changing amoeba-like shape, suddenly elongated as one or two try to escape, then settling back, becoming fatter as the activity subsides, but disintegrating into total chaos in the closing moments—these are strange sights indeed to the uninitiated.

Yet people—men and women alike—have been racing on bicycles since the moment they appeared on the scene. Official races took place within five years of the production of Pierre Michaux's first velocipedes. Informal racing had been in progress from the moment that two velocipedists first found themselves side by side. As bike racing took hold it began to take on various forms. Long, inter-city races were held. Special tracks were built. People raced against all manner of things, not just other people on bicycles: carriages, trotting horses, railroad trains.

Some long-lasting patterns were established in the early years of the cycle-racing fever. The Paris–Rouen race of 1869 set the tone for the French preoccupation with long-distance contests. In England cycle racers ran afoul of the law and of public opinion early on and adandoned large, "massed start" races in favor of individual "time trialing." Americans gravitated to horse racing and trotting tracks and later to specially built board cycle tracks. Track racing events remained our forte for better than three decades.

Not many people are aware, today, that bicycle racing was ever prominent in this country. It may come as a surprise to many that American riders dominated world compe-

tition in track-racing events for a long period of time and cycle racing was practically the national sport.

The first American cyclist to reach world-class status was Arthur Augustus Zimmerman, known to his innumerable fans as "Zimmy." Zimmy became a professional in 1894, after winning just about every amateur contest in sight, including the five- and fifty-mile championships of England in '92 and the one-mile and ten-mile titles in the first World Cycling meet held in Chicago the following year. Zimmerman went on to race both at home and abroad—in Britain, on the Continent, and in Australia—with great success, drawing what for those days were huge crowds, sometimes approaching 30,000 fans.

Following Zimmerman came another international champion, Marshall "Major" Taylor, a black American from Indianapolis. Taylor was a sprinter par excellence and his professional career lasted more than fifteen years, most of it spent abroad, where he is still much better known than he is in this country.

The list of American champions of this era (particularly from the mid-'90s to the end of the 1920s) is lengthy, but two more certainly deserve mention: Bobby Walthour, the "Dixie Flyer"; and Frank Kramer, perhaps the greatest of them all. Walthour was an all-around cyclist, winning everything from sprints to six-day races. Kramer, like so many of the American cyclists, was primarily a sprinter and track racer. Kramer broke into professional cycle racing in 1900, when, as a complete unknown, he took second to Major Taylor in the national sprint championships. During the twenty-two years of his succeeding career, Kramer was to be sprint champion eighteen times. Sixteen of those titles were won in consecutive years. Though he was successful abroad Kramer spent the greater part of his career at home, where he was revered on a level comparable to Babe Ruth,

Jack Dempsey and Bobby Jones—the other sports "superheroes" of the time. Kramer was a star in every sense. He had that presence that commands respect. His austere and disciplined lifestyle was an irreproachable model for people young and old alike.

It is thought by many that Kramer's stature and charisma were solely responsible for keeping cycle racing alive in the United States for its last decade or so, because within a relatively short time after his retirement in 1922 the sport virtually disappeared, leaving the velodromes deserted. The crowds simply went on to other forms of entertainment and the American presence in world bicycle racing dwindled to nothing.

EUROPEAN ROAD RACING

On the Continent things had taken a somewhat different turn. There was track racing, of course, and it was hotly contested, but the imagination of Europeans (most especially the French) was captured by long-distance, intercity road racing. The 123-kilometer Paris–Rouen race of 1869 served as the model. It was followed in the next decade by the establishment of a 572-kilometer race from Bordeaux to Paris and 1,280-kilometer (!) event running from Paris to Brest and back to Paris. (The Paris–Brest–Paris race is still run every nine years or so, and is still one of the most formidable one-stage road races anywhere.)

Much was learned about the limits of human endurance in these contests (for example, that some people can pedal for days on end with very little or no rest but that they need to eat as they go). Contrary to the predictions of skeptics who said that no competitors would attempt to race over such distances, the races attracted large fields of contestants and became regular events.

Other now-classic long-distance road races were instituted in France and neighboring countries before the turn of the century, including the Paris–Roubaix, Paris–Tours, Liège–Bastogne–Liège, and Paris–Brussels contests; but the "race to end all races," the *Tour de France,* was not born until 1903.

In that year Henri Desgranges, editor of *L'Auto,* a motoring and cycling weekly, was casting about for a scheme to boost the circulation of his periodical when he hit on the idea of a sort of glorified six-day race over the roads of France. This was the seed. As it took root it blossomed into the outrageous notion of "circum-cycling" the entire perimeter of France in a series of stages—a concept so grandiose that the almost universal reaction was of skepticism and disbelief.

Desgranges persisted in the face of ridicule, and actually succeeded in getting the monumental event off the ground. The first *Tour*, very much like present-day versions, lasted a bit over a month, with the individual stages of the race averaging about 400 kilometers each. (Unlike more recent *Tours* there were many days of rest included in the schedule.)

Despite the mood of doubt that accompanied the beginning of the race, by the time it was nearing its end the contest had generated such a fever pitch of excitement among the public that the reaction must have exceeded even Desgranges' wildest hopes. It was, in short, a resounding success. Such was the enthusiasm and partisanship of the public that a lot of foul play (on the part of the fans) took place in subsequent *Tours*, nearly causing the event to be banned. Good sense returned, however (along with some altered planning that diminished the likelihood of such unsportsmanlike conduct), and the *Tour de France* became firmly established as a sporting event to "end all."

In the next decade, other "tours" were started in imitation of *the* Tour: of Italy (the *Giro d'Italia*), Belgium (the *Tour de Flandres*), and Spain (the *Vuelta de España*). These, along with the *Tour de France* and the aforementioned inter-city classics, make up the heart of European summertime cycling competition. They are generally considered to be the supreme test of a cyclist's abilities, combining every type of terrain and climate— from wet, jarring cobblestone streets; to snowy, virtually unpaved mountain passes; to long, hot, dusty stretches of rural roads—into an efficient torture device for cyclists.

SIX-DAY RACING

The indoor event that served as the inspiration for the *Tour de France*, the so-called six-day race, originated in Britain in 1881. The idea was simple, if grim. Racers rode round and round a small board track continuously for six days—or for as much of the six days as consciousness could be maintained. The six-day duration wasn't decided on arbitrarily; it was determined by the "blue laws" that forbade sporting contests (as well as drinking and a large number of other things) on Sunday. It was the maximum uninterrupted portion of time that was possible to string together without offending the Lord.

Interestingly, six-day racing grew out of a then-current fad: roller-skating. Roller-rink operators, seeking a diversion to maintain interest in skating, first hired cyclists to ride around the outsides of the tracks on which the skaters were gyrating. In the end the bicycles became the center of attention and the skaters vanished. The spectators were there for excitement, naturally, and as their demands for more exciting action grew, tracks were redesigned with higher banking on the turns and the races grew longer—right up to the limits noted above.

While the practice of six-day racing was abandoned fairly soon after its "invention" in Britain, it quickly caught on in the United States where it was carried on with great enthusiasm in a number of arenas, but most especially Madison Square Garden. Six-day races are still known in Europe by the term "Madison" that was coined in this era. In 1899 head-to-head six-day racing was outlawed for humanitarian reasons, and replaced by a new style in which two-man teams competed. The change proved to be beneficial for riders and fans alike. The race became more than just an incredibly endless endurance contest, with people riding themselves into insensibility around the tiny track. The pace quickened and action was stimulated by a number of devices, such as offering extra points and/or prizes at intervals during the race. (The basic scoring move in this style of racing is overlapping the opponent.)

Six-day bicycle racing in its new form remained a very popular spectator sport in this country through the first two decades of the century, but, as noted, died out quite suddenly and completely along with all other forms of professional cycling. In Europe, however, professional racing remained alive; six-day racing has been carried on continuously, offering a winter alternative to road racing. Modern six-day racing generally involves six consecutive *evenings* of hard team racing with a variety of events, including such eye-openers as motor-paced sprints, prearranged "jams," and chases to keep up the excitement level. Points are awarded along the way according to a predetermined scheme.

MODERN TRACK RACING

Official cycle competition, international style, is divided into track and road events. The basic track event is the "match" sprint (or just "sprint")—a head-to-head confrontation between two riders over a distance of 1,000 meters. This, by the way, is the event that Americans like Zimmerman, Taylor, and Kramer dominated in the years between the 1890s and the 1920s.

In the match sprint only the last 200 meters of the race is timed. The earlier part of the race is generally a battle of wits, with

Bicycles were big business at the turn of the century—as they are today. Then, as now, technical sophistication was one of the attributes that makers relied upon to make their products attractive to the public—but not the only one.

Women took to cycling almost as soon as men, participating in most of the earliest official races. Women held records in racing over both long and short distances and in long-distance tour activities.

Professional cycle racing was a popular spectator sport in its early days; even more, it was a polite entertainment for the well-to-do, rather like the Ascot races are for present-day Britons. At velodromes on the Continent and in the States, considerable comforts were available to the patrons, while for the rider, the demands of the six-day ordeal were almost inhuman.

The peloton or pack is the basic "organism" of road racing. Like an amoeba, it changes shape constantly in response to different stimuli.

In order to win, a rider must endeavor to break away from the peloton—to open up a decisive lead. What usually happens is that several riders attempt this at the same time, forming a miniature peloton or "breakaway group."

An altogether different type of racing: the match sprint—a quintessential head-to-head battle of strength and tactics.

These two bicycles were designed and built in the workshops of former racers: Cino Cinelli, a seminal figure in the Italian bike-building and racing world, and Eddy Merckx, probably the most famous and successful all-around road racer of all time.

Sante Pogliaghi is thought of by many as the "patron saint" of track racers. Considerable mystique surrounds his bicycles—both track and road models. Pogliaghi's frames are produced in small numbers, almost entirely under his direct supervision.

This 'Team' bike by the distinguished English builder Ron Cooper is a finely crafted product involving much personal handwork. It teams some of the most sophisticated Japanese components with more familiar Italian ones and it sports truly unusual laminated wooden rims.

both riders trying to maneuver the opponent into a disadvantageous position. Contrary to the obvious expectation, the preferred position is usually *behind* the opponent. In the past this jockeying for position sometimes lasted so long (thirty minutes or more) that regulations now limit the duration of the overall contest.

Once one of the contestants decides that the time is ripe, he or she initiates the sprint proper and the race is on. As mentioned, most sprinters prefer to be behind the opponent at the onset of the final dash. From the rear position a rider has the opponent in full view and can make a pretty accurate assessment of his or her reserve capacities. Also, the rider in front is working harder, breaking the force of wind resistance for the follower, who tries to gauge the most favorable moment in which to flash past for victory.

Another track event is the pursuit race. In the pursuits, usually run over a distance of 4,000 meters, the two riders start on opposite sides of the velodrome and attempt to overtake each other. (This strikes me as one of the most fiendish motivational devices ever generated by the human brain.) A rider who is successfully overtaken automatically loses the race. But since this seldom happens (riders in big-time competition are usually far too evenly matched) the race is timed and the laurels go to the faster rider.

In team pursuit competition four-man teams play out the same drama as the solo riders in the individual pursuit. Team members rotate positions, each taking his or her turn at the head, pacing the team and taking the brunt of the air resistance, then falling back to the back of the pack in turn. A good pursuit team operates like a well-oiled machine. It is fast, precise, and rhythmical. Nothing is wasted. The moves must be second nature and the team must respond like a single organism to the progress of the race.

The one other track event commonly held in international competition is the 1,000-meter time trial: one rider racing against the clock from a standing start. At the gun the racer must get into motion unassisted, whereupon the problem is one of judging pace or the expenditure of energy over the 1,000 meters. Winning times in international competition are under 1¼ minutes. It may not sound (or look) like much of an event, but the popular wisdom is that it is perhaps the roughest. It is often said that it takes the better part of a week for a rider to fully recover from the strain of a truly well-pedaled kilometer time trial.

MODERN ROAD RACING

There are different types of road races, though they are not as specifically defined as official track events. There is the criterium, which consists of many, many laps around a comparatively short course, usually one to three kilometers, usually on the streets of a city or town. The point-to-point or out-and-back long-distance race, typified by the European classics, is another type. Then there is the stage race, carried on over a number of days (or weeks) and in which each separate stage may consist of a point-to-point, a criterium, or a time trial.

Road races are massed-start races, unlike most track events which pit one contestant or small team against another. Winning a road race is rather like trying to escape from a magnetic field. It is difficult to escape from the field to begin with and, even if you manage it, your very energy tends to pull the rest of the mass right along behind you.

The mass or pack of riders is called the *peloton* (French for squadron). The peloton has a pace and a life of its own—a sort of collective consciousness. To win the race, or at least to gain the lead, it is necessary to break away from the peloton. An attempted break sets in motion a chain reaction. The pace quickens and the peloton, this collective animal, strives to reabsorb the escaping rider or riders. Sometimes it is a single rider who dares to break from the pack. More often it is a group of riders—either several team members by pre-arrangement or a mixed group consisting of riders who simply decided to jump at the same moment—or a leader and several pursuers. If the pack does succeed in catching the break (as it often does), the "attackers" will be swallowed up by the peloton and often "blown right out the back," since their effort is likely to have taken a heavy toll in terms of their energy reserves.

Tactics in road racing is a large subject. There are two basic tactical alternatives. You can either take the lead early and try to hold it—a very risky and taxing option—or you can stay with the peloton for most of the race and choose the most advantageous moment at which to make your move. (The latter is the strategy most often chosen.) The situation becomes complicated, naturally. Suppose, for example, that you choose Alternative Two while another rider or riders choose Alternative One. Choices are sometimes dictated by circumstances and the actions of others may foreclose options.

One of the main tactical realities is that bicycle road racing has become a team sport. It didn't start out that way; regulations don't specify teams. Teams don't win races—individuals do (at least as far as the public is concerned). Yet it would be foolish to contend that the unsupported individual has much of a chance in big-time road races. An extraordinary individual like the great Belgian racer Eddy Merkx could get away with taking a stage—or two—or three—on sheer guts, but to hope realistically for victory in a race like the *Tour de France,* a rider must have the support of a well-organized, well-disciplined team.

A team is generally built around a key member—a star performer—and its purpose is to get that rider to the finish line first. Two pieces of racing strategy that involve teamwork are the "lead-out," in which the team or some members of the team break together, so as to be able to share the pacing tasks (usually allowing the team leader the opportunity to put it all together at the end) and "blocking." When the team leader or star makes a break, some or all of the peloton will naturally try to follow. If team members can succeed in making further escape from the pack impossible for a time, the breaker has a better chance of opening up a commanding lead. If the team leader is unlucky enough to have a puncture or a mechanical breakdown, team members (known as *domestiques* on the European circuit) will hand over their machines, if appropriate, or will at the very least stay with the disabled star and pace him back into the peloton after repairs are completed.

(It seems to strike many people that this arrangement, wherein a group of fine athletes makes their identities and interests subservient to those of a favored star, is somehow inconsistent with the individual spirit of bicycle racing. But the name of the game here, as elsewhere, is winning. It is a profession as well as a sport and team members are well paid for their efforts, if successful. The help of teammates and teamwork are recognized in the common gesture made by *Tour* winners of giving *all* the prize money to the supporting cast.)

There are, of course, countless subtleties of racing tactics, such as the best time to stage a break (one strategy that has been employed with success in recent years is waiting for the moment at which another attempted break has been caught or prevented—a moment of letdown and fatigue for many riders in the peloton), but those are the subject for a different sort of book.

AMERICAN RENAISSANCE

Bicycle racing, of course, continued in this country after the demise of professional (one might almost say commercial) competition, but almost exclusively on an amateur basis. Americans competed only against other Americans in a system set up by the United States Cycling Federation, the governing body of U.S. amateur racing.

The U.S.C.F. licenses amateur men and women bicycle riders (plus a few professionals) according to a system of age categories, further subdivided in the main senior category into classifications based on experience and achievement. It is a neat, equitable, orderly system, typical of U.S. amateur athletic organizations.

Over the years the most important U.S.C.F. racing has been the District and National Championships. Each year in June, championships in both road and track events are held in each of the forty-nine U.S.C.F. jurisdictions or Districts. The winners from the District Championships go on to compete in the National meet held a month or two later.

Any U.S.C.F. licensed rider may participate in the District meets, thus it is this racing that involves the greatest number of cyclists.

Another U.S.C.F. event is the National Classic Series, a prescheduled roster of road races spread over the summertime racing season with varying numbers of points awarded to the first ten finishers in each race. At the end of the Series, the high-point scorer is the National Classic Champion.

Besides the running of the intranational cycle racing scene, the Federation, through its affiliations with the U.S. Amateur Athletic Union (A.A.U.) and the *Union Cycliste Internationale* (U.I.C.), its international counterpart, has a hand in selecting and running all the major international cycling competitions: the Olympic Games, the Pan-American Games, and the World Cycling Championships. To this end, in order to help select teams for these events, the Federation sponsors one additional race series in the appropriate years. The International Development Series, a point-system event much like the

Classic Series, helps coaches gather information about U.S. riders and their potential as U.S. team members.

The Pan-American Games of 1975 marked a new departure for U.S. competitors, who had commanded little or no respect from the international racing set for the previous few decades. At the '75 Pan-Am meet the American sprint champion, Steve Woznick, took the gold medal in the 1,000-meter match event. Perhaps more unexpected and thus inspiring was the victory of the American pursuit team, which snatched victory from the heavily favored Colombian foursome in what will be long remembered as a high point in U.S. cycle-racing history. The United States was back in the running, so to speak.

Interestingly enough in the ensuing half-decade since the '75 Pan-Am Games, it has been the American *women*, who have had the greatest success in international competition. The reasons for this are a subject of some speculation but the consensus is more or less as follows. First, we start from a cultural perspective in which theoretical equality among women and men is more widely accepted than in many other societies. Next, despite the truth of the first premise, there have been virtually no facilities made available to female cycle racers in this country. As a result, the serious women racers here have been more or less forced to train with the men.

However speculative the explanation, the successes have been real enough. The new era for American women actually began years before the victories at the Pan-Am Games, and was ushered in by a virtual unknown. Audrey McElmury arrived at the World Cycling Championships in Brno, Czechoslovakia, in October 1969 without any of the acoutrements, assistance, recognition, or fanfare that usually accompany successful riders on the Continent. She left Brno as World Road-Racing Champion (female variety) after a ride

that was, to say the least, dramatic. McElmury crashed in her attempt to shake the peloton on the last lap of the race. She remounted, bleeding, and succeeded in regaining contact with the pack. In a final burst of determination and courage she broke away a second time, on the final hill, to claim victory by a substantial margin.

Audrey McElmury's first place finish in the Worlds was indeed a first for an American of either sex (for more than half a century). Her achievement attracted more attention in Europe where it was more fully comprehended than it did in the United States, but it certainly did not hurt the chances of other American women who came after her.

And come they did. In 1973 Sheila Young (who, with her brother Roger, had managed to keep both the women's and men's U.S. National Sprint Championships in the same family) went to the Worlds and came away World Sprint Champion. American Sue Novara claimed that title in 1975. In 1980 Novara reclaimed her '75 title and Beth Heiden (a relative newcomer to the cycle-racing scene, which she has dominated since her arrival) brought back the gold medal in the road competition. American women are now racing in international events with a bit more support and recognition.

The 1980 World Cycling Championships, while certainly a high-water mark for U.S. women, provided some encouraging indications of headway for the men as well. Jacques Boyer, one of the few professional American cycle racers, made a fine bid in the men's professional road race (which was ultimately taken by the *1979 Tour de France* winner Bernard Hinault). Boyer hung in with the scant fifteen of the original 160 starters who managed to finish the race and, narrowly missing a bid for third or fourth place, nevertheless posted the highest finishing position of any American in recent history (fifth).

Boyer races regularly on the European

circuit, one of the few American riders who has found it possible to withstand the blistering pace and absolutely relentless competition of European cycle racing. The experience has paid off for Boyer and he, in turn, has proved that Americans are capable of competing at the levels set by the legendary French, Belgian, Spanish, and Italian riders for whom it was not only a sport but the best "job" they were ever likely to get.

American *teams* will begin to experience international success on the professional circuit when, and only when, the sport becomes popular enough to generate the commercial support that it enjoys abroad. Although cycle racing is a long way from displacing the Super Bowl as America's most important sporting event, the seeds of change have been planted. American business has begun to discover that rewards and recognition can come from sponsoring competition in cycle racing as well as in tennis and golf. The more prize money and prestige available on American race courses, the more qualified athletes there will be on hand to compete for them.

Of course competition isn't the whole story in winning performances. There is coaching too. A winning racer is a smart, seasoned cyclist. One of the interesting facts about American cycle racing in the last decade or so is the unusual number of successful riders who have emerged from family-structured training programs. A surprising number of the younger breed of U.S. racers who have achieved notable success over these years have been sibling pairs (or, in one case, a quartet).

Sheila and Roger Young have been mentioned. In 1973 this sister-brother combination managed to capture both the women's and men's National Sprint titles. Roger is still an active racer, a member of the 1980 gold-medal-winning U.S. time-trial team at the Pan-American Games. Sheila now coaches.

The Stetina family has given the United States a virtual dynasty of bicycle racers. Father Roy and mother Janice Stetina were quite successful in their years as a husband-and-wife racing team in Ohio. Their experience and enthusiasm has gone into making champions out of their four sons. The two elder brothers, Dale and Wayne, have been competing with continuing success for several years, both at home and abroad. Younger brothers Joel and Troy have been coming up through the ranks of the juniors—and looking very good.

The most recent family act in American bicycle racing is the Kenosha, Wisconsin, Heiden duo who made history at the 1980 Winter Olympics at Lake Placid, New York. Brother Eric set a world precedent by winning *five* gold medals in the speed-skating competition. Sister Beth, who won the bronze medal in the 3,000-meter skating event, so far has outclassed her brother as a cycle racer. In 1980 Beth emerged as a clear dominating force in women's cycle racing by winning, among others, the U.S.C.F. National title, the Coors Classic, and the World Road Championship. Eric, who had not actually competed as a cyclist before Lake Placid, has dedicated himself to this new sport and holds much promise for the future.

The frame has been characterized by various writers on the subject as the "skeleton" of the bicycle, the "heart" of the bicycle, the "most important part" of the bicycle. Perhaps a better way to get the point across would be to say that, in a sense, the frame *is* the bicycle. The other parts are necessary, of course—the wheels, the handlebars, the saddle—and depending on their selection, they will affect the bicycle's performance in various ways. But *most* of how a bicycle will behave is built right into the frame.

ANATOMY OF A HIGH-TECH FRAME

Of all the processes that go into creating a bicycle, frame building has proved the least susceptible to the techniques of mass production. All the finest bicycle frames are hand built by carefully trained craftsmen. There are several reasons for this. Some have to do with the nature of the materials involved and how they must be handled; some have to do with the shape of the frame and its relation to the shape of the rider. (These will be discussed at greater length later.) In any case, a fine bicycle frame is one of the few items around these days that *is* still made by hand. This makes them expensive, but a skillfully made frame is a work of art as well as a utilitarian object.

As there is reputed to be more than one way to skin a cat, there is certainly more than one way to understand a bicycle. To gain an intuitive understanding you have only to get on your bike and ride it, whereupon you will rapidly come to know what it feels like and what it is capable of doing.

Another approach is to examine each part, to see how and why it functions and how its function relates to the functioning of the whole. It's what medical students do in the first stages of their training. Before that active anatomical study begins, however, each first-year medical student spends hundreds of hours studying what is called gross anatomy: memorizing the names of the thousands of parts, structures, and systems that make up the human body. After all an intelligent discussion requires that all the participants agree upon the terms they use.

In the same sense, in order for us to talk about bicycles clearly, we will need to agree on some basic anatomical vocabulary. Fortunately the bicycle is a simple organism compared with the human body and since the design of conventional bicycles has been largely standardized for quite a while, the task will not be difficult.

Let's begin our dissection with the frame. We'll examine all the components that attach to the frame afterward.

THE NAMING OF PARTS, I

Starting from the front of the bicycle frame, the first structure we see is known as the front **fork**, and it does bear a remote resemblance to the eating utensil or the tool used to pitch hay. The axle of the wheel fits into the shaped **fork ends** or **dropouts** at the ends of the curved, more or less upright fork **blades**. The blades are attached at the top to each other and to the **steering column** or **tube** by means of a bridge called the **fork crown**. (Unless you assemble or dismantle your own bicycle, you may never actually see the steering tube.) The steering tube is housed within another tube, known as the **head tube**, which is part of the main structure of the frame. Supporting the steering column within the head tube are two ball-bearing assemblies, top and bottom, known as the **head bearings** or,

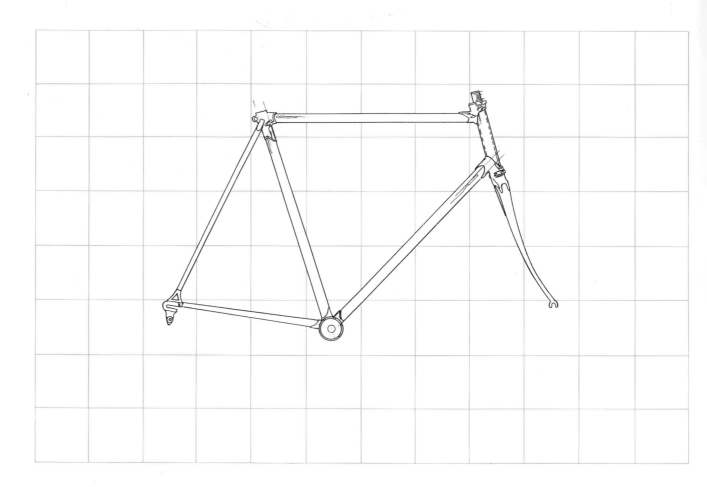

collectively, as the **head set.**

Connected to the head tube are the horizontal **top tube** and the downward-slanting **down tube**. Completing the **main triangle** of the **frame** is the **seat tube**, running more or less parallel to the head tube and so called because the seat or saddle is anchored to it by means of the **seat post** that fits inside the top of the tube.

The joints between the various tubes making up the main triangle are reinforced (in most fine bicycles) by thin, specially shaped sleeves called **lugs**. While lugs may also have ornamental value (indeed, neatly executed lugwork is one of the hallmarks of a finely made bicycle), their primary purpose is to provide extra material and extra surface for the brazing or joining material—they strengthen the tube joints.

At the bottom of the triangle, at the junction of the seat tube and the down tube, is the structure variously known as the **crank axle housing, crank hanger,** or, most often, the **bottom bracket shell.** In a sense it is a glorified lug, but it has considerably more significance than any of the other lugs. In fact it is one of the most critical structures of the whole frame. As its name suggests, it is the tunnel through which the main axle, the part that connects the pedal cranks, runs; it is where most of the stresses of pedaling are exerted on the frame—where the power is transferred from the rider to the machine. It takes more abuse than any other part of the bicycle.

The **rear** or **secondary triangle** is made up of two pairs of **stays** (in addition to the seat tube—which, geometrically speaking, makes up one side of it); the more or less horizontal **chain stays** and the more or less vertical **seat stays.** The chain stays attach at the front to the bottom bracket shell. The seat stays connect to the seat lug (the lug at the joint of the top tube and the seat tube) to form the **seat cluster.** The two sets of stays join to form two triangles by means of the **rear dropouts,** which accommodate the axle of the rear wheel. Rear dropouts are made in different configurations, depending on the design and the intended use of the bicycle.

This, then, completes the basic anatomy of the bicycle frame.

BASIC BICYCLE FRAME GEOMETRY

To the eye of the uninitiated, most bicycle frames look pretty much alike. Even to the eye of the fanatic the differences are subtle, but the fact is that frames vary both in size and in shape. The working out of a frame design has two main objectives. First, the rider's weight is distributed over the frame in a fairly precise manner, which will vary depending on the use of the bicycle. Second, the points of contact between the rider and the machine—the saddle, the handlebars, and the pedals—have to be arranged physically to coincide with the shape of the rider and in a configuration that makes for an efficient transfer of power from the "engine" to the machine. In the most general terms the dimensions that have to do with how the bike is stretched out horizontally largely determine the performance characteristics of the bike (and hence its use). The dimensions that determine how tall it is are largely related to the size of the rider. These are very broad generalizations, however. All the dimensions and other design factors are interrelated. In fact, considering how simple the geometry of the "diamond" frame appears, the problems of

The extreme limits of bottom bracket height in conventional bike building practice.

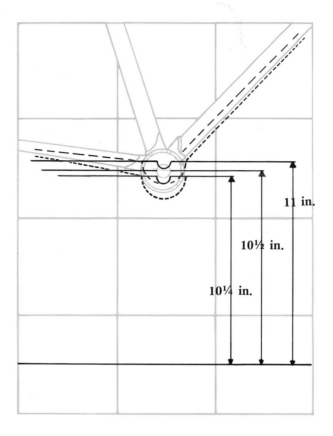

11 in.

10½ in.

10¼ in.

frame design are surprisingly complicated (but not too complicated to talk about).

The design of the diamond frame has been worked out so thoroughly over the years that overall improvements are no longer a realistic possibility. What we have learned is that the basic design offers a range of variables or trade-offs and the builder chooses among them to create a bike suited to a specific purpose. By changing one element we can make a bike to *this* better. By altering that tube angle we can improve *that* characteristic, but usually at the expense of something else. The actual range of many of the variables is quite small and seemingly minor changes in dimensions and geometry make for very significant alterations in the way a bike behaves.

Here's how it works. There is only one constant, one invariable starting point for any

conventional bicycle frame: the diameter of the wheels. This determines how far off the ground the fork tips and the rear dropouts will be. Everything else about the frame is a matter of deliberate design choice.

The bottom bracket is the center of gravity of the bicycle and, all things being equal, it should be kept as low as possible for the sake of stability. But its closeness to the ground is limited by the fact that the pedals have to clear the ground—not only in pedaling on the straightaways, but in cornering too. So here is the first trade-off: lower center of gravity, less pedal clearance; more pedal clearance, less stability. The builder makes a choice based on the intended use of the bicycle.

Once that choice is made the designer must decide on the overall wheelbase for the bicycle—how far the wheel axles will be from the bottom bracket and from each other. Factors influencing this decision are the need for wheel clearance and a number of things having to do with the ride and handling characteristics of the bike. For safety's sake the front wheel must clear pedals and toe clips. The rear wheel can be only as close to the bottom bracket as the presence of the seat tube allows. In addition the user may require more space still, to fit mudguards and/or to provide clearance between his or her heel and panniers or other luggage. In the ride and handling department bikes with short wheelbases tend to accelerate more rapidly and have a "nervous" feel. Long-wheelbase designs tend to be slower, but more stable and comfortable. One final consideration is that shorter chain stays correlate with increased overall rigidity of the frame—its ability to resist lateral flexing produced by powerful pedaling.

By time-honored tradition the "size" of a bicycle is the measurement of the length of the seat tube, and this is determined in relation to the length of the rider's leg. There are a number of different formulas for determining the specific relationship between the two, and we will take a look at some of them later. Suffice to say here that the dimension of the seat tube is a matter related to the size of the person who is expected to ride the bike.

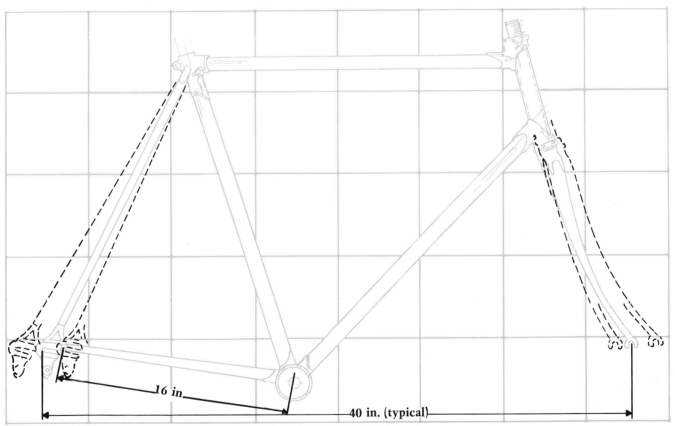

16 in.

40 in. (typical)

The longest and shortest wheelbases found on conventional bicycles are 44 inches and 38 inches respectively.

The "average" is about 40 inches. Chain stay lengths vary between 16 and 18 inches.

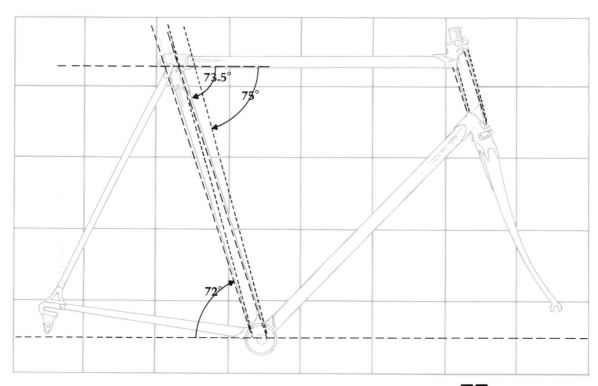

Head and seat tube angles vary between 75° (the steepest) and 72° (the shallowest). Most bikes stay close to the mean (73.5°). Varying these angles affects top tube length.

The *angle* of the seat tube is one of the more critical variables as far as weight distribution is concerned, since it controls to some extent the rider's front-to-back position. It also has a profound effect on the ride of the bicycle. The steeper the angle the more road shock and vibration is transmitted. The shallower the angle, the more is absorbed.

Along with the angle of the seat tube, the angle of the head tube is a critical design feature in terms of geometry. The head-tube angle is the bicycle's steering axis and this, in combination with the amount of bend or "rake" in the fork blades, determines how the bike will steer. The steeper the head-tube angle (the closer to the vertical), the more road shock will be transmitted to the rider's hands and wrists. The shallower the angle, the more will be absorbed. Also the steeper the angle, the more maneuverable the bike but the harder to control. The head angle and the fork rake combine to determine the amount of "trail" in the steering design. The amount of trail is the distance between where the steering axis intersects the ground and the place where the wheel actually makes contact. The latter point is always *behind* the former, hence the term trail. The more trail a bike

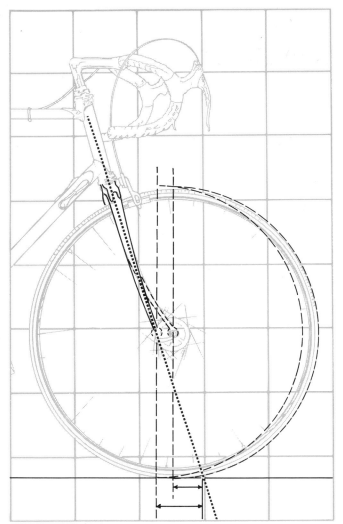

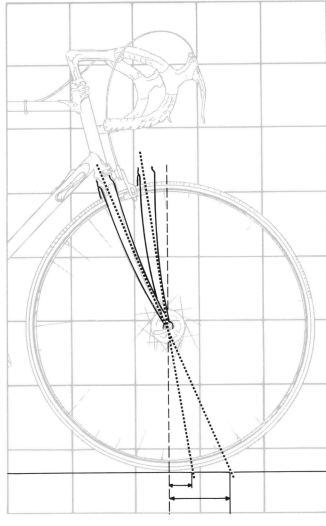

As fork rake (off-
set) increases,
trail decreases.

The shallower the
head angle, the
greater the amount of
trail; the steeper the
angle, the less trail.

has, the more stable its steering; the more it
will tend to keep moving in a straight line, to
resist turning.

Once decisions about head angle and
fork rake have been made, the builder is
pretty close to the end of the basic designing

process. All that remains is to determine the
dimensions of the top tube and the down
tube. Here you begin to see the ways in
which the different elements are interrelated.
If the dimensions and angles of all the parts
we have discussed so far are determined, then

the length of the top tube has also been determined, as a function of the overall wheelbase. Ideally speaking the length of the top tube should be determined by the upper body and arm length of the rider. In a custom-made, "cut-to-fit" frame this should certainly be the case. So top-tube length becomes a factor in determining the wheelbase. It may also influence the angle of the seat tube. The only frame component that does not have much importance in terms of its influence on how the bike *works* is the down tube. It is simply placed so as to join the head tube to the bottom bracket while giving an adequate amount of clearance to the front wheel.

So there it is in a nutshell. There are lots of variables. It is interesting, however, to note how very limited the actual, physical range of variation is for most of these factors. A touring bicycle, for example, where the main consideration is keeping a low center of gravity for maximum stability, will most likely have a bottom bracket with the pedal axle centered about 10¼ inches above the ground. A sprint bike built for maximum pedal clearance from the steeply banked racing track will have the highest bottom bracket; 11 inches off the ground. That is a total variable of ¾ inch. Chain-stay length is another of the variables that is quite limited. The range within which bicycles work satisfactorily is between 16 and 18 inches. The vast majority of bicycles have chain stays between 16½ and 17½ inches. Differences in tube angles (for recent designs of handmade bicycles) run from the shallowest angles of 72° to the most "radical" angles (the steepest) of 75°—a total range of 3°. Even the range of overall wheelbases is fairly limited, running from a maximum of about 44 inches for a "stretched out" touring bike down to about 38 inches for a "tight" sprint or pursuit bike—a total difference of no more than 6 inches.

A CLOSER LOOK

With all this in mind let us review our anatomy lesson, but in a bit more detail this time.

THE FORK

The front fork is made up of six elements, which may all come from different manufacturers: the crown, the steering column, two blades, and two ends or tips—with the possible addition of reinforcing "tangs" welded to the crown to give more support to the tops of the fork blades.

Starting from the bottom up, the fork tips, of all the numerous bits and pieces of the bicycle seem to generate the least amount of controversy. Both forged and cast tips are produced by several manufacturers and are generally considered to be of comparable quality.

A little farther up, the fork blades are a

These forged racing fork tips by Campagnolo have been drilled out by the builder (Raleigh) for maximum weight saving.

subject of considerable controversy. The cross section of the tubing used depends on the type of bicycle: track bikes have round fork blades; road bikes, oval. The reason for the latter is that the action of braking puts a lot of fore-and-aft stress on the blades, which brakeless track bike forks do not have to contend with. The oval section increases the ability of the fork blades to withstand braking stresses.

Tubes for fork blades are a bit different from standard frame tubes. In fact there are two widely accepted specially designed fork blade tubes. TI Reynolds, the pioneer in the field, devised a fork tube that is not only butted in the normal sense, but which tapers in wall thickness toward the tip as the tube diminishes in section. The theory here is that most of the stress occurs at the point of joining—the top. Most of the resilience, the ability to flex and absorb road shock, comes into play in the curved or raked portion of the

blade; having less metal down there allows the blades to act more like springs.

The Italian tube-making firm of A.L. Colombo, which got into the game a good thirty years after Reynolds, worked out the problem differently. The Columbus (as the firm is referred to here) fork blade is of tapering section but consistent wall thickness. It is also larger in overall section than the Reynolds fork blade and rounder. The so-called Italian or continental section blade has considerably more lateral rigidity than the Reynolds design, so goes the consensus. That is, it resists the sideward stresses generated in cornering. (Interestingly, it has become so popular that Reynolds now makes its own "Italian section" fork blade.)

The fork crown has taken on a surprising number of forms, considering the simplicity of its functions—which are to connect the fork blades strongly and reliably to the steering column and, secondarily, to serve as a

mounting platform for the front brake. Flat fork crowns, the most common type, are the least rugged, the easiest to make (they are stamped and welded) and hence the least expensive. They are rarely used on handmade bicycles nowadays. The fully sloping crown, developed by the Italian frame-builder and component-manufacturer Cino Cinelli, is cast, heavy and virtually indestructable. The Cinelli or Cinelli-style crown is unique in that its design requires the fork blade to slip *over* the mounting sleeve, rather than *inside,* the more usual procedure. This is a subject of controversy, as the heat applied in brazing thus primarily affects the metal of the blade itself rather than the mounting tang or sleeve—or so many builders feel. The semi-sloping crown was the inevitable compromise between the old, flat style and the massive Cinelli style. It is much stronger than the former and considerably lighter than the latter. Most semi-sloping crowns are designed to accommodate the Columbus-style fork blade.

Long reinforcing tangs are added to the crown by a number of builders. The idea is that more surface area will make a stronger

joint between crown and blade. There is no consensus on this question. Many other builders point out that, in effect, the tangs are merely brazed onto the sides of the fork blades adding nothing but decoration. In any case enough of the finest builders omit their use so that no one need be concerned about not having them.

The one invisible part of your bicycle is the steering tube. For all that you can't see it, it takes a lot of punishment. Many steering tubes are straight gauge steel tubes, but not all. A Columbus tube set includes a specially designed steerer that is both butted and strengthened with internal reinforcing ridges so that it is extremely resistant to torsional forces but remains relatively light. The head bearings that suspend the steering tube within the head tube are the subject of considerable experimentation, although their function is simple. The problem is that they need to be tough, but people would rather do without a lot of weight here. So a number of manufacturers have devoted their ingenuity to reducing weight without diminishing performance. The general solution seems to be to make the

Fork crown styles (clockwise, from upper left). Flat crown (custom, Speedwell); typical cast semi-sloping crown; Cinelli fully sloping cast crown; an aerodynamic version of the fully sloping crown (Rossin).

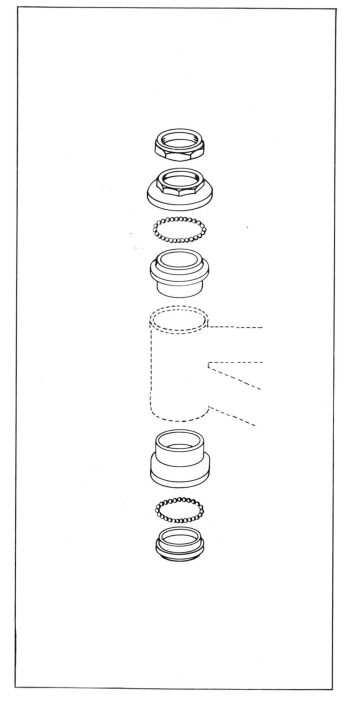

Typical head bearing assembly (head set) consisting of cups, cones, balls, and locknuts.

housings and all the non-bearing surfaces out of forged and heat-treated aluminum alloy and attaching hardened steel "races" or bearing surfaces for the steel balls to run in. The Campagnolo Super Record head set is of this type and, as with most of Campagnolo's products, it is the standard by which others are measured. There are, of course, other head sets worthy of consideration. First of all not everyone needs the weight reduction (at twice the price) offered by aluminum alloy in place of steel—hence the Campagnolo Record steel head set and its many imitators. On the other hand some racers will go for minimum weight at any cost. The Italian firm O.M.A.S. manufactures a line of head sets in which the housings and races are entirely of aluminum alloy. The O.M.A.S. head set uses smaller than normal ball bearings to distribute the load more evenly over the bearing surfaces. Several sealed-bearing head sets have appeared on the scene in the past few years. The Avocet Model III is an interesting example. It uses a system of cylindrical rollers, oriented at cross angles, in place of the standard balls. This makes for a super-strong bearing at a reasonable weight.

As with all parts of the frame, the technique of the builder is a significant factor in determining the strength and hence the quality of the finished fork. Even given the best materials and components, the fork can be rendered vulnerable to sudden failure by careless application of heat; rapid and uneven cooling can warp the assembly. For the finest possible result each step has to be carried out with care.

THE MAIN TRIANGLE

The main triangle (in reality a trapezoid or irregular quadrangle in shape) receives the most attention of any portion of the bicycle. It is a simple structure but it does a big job, acting as a central distribution system for human-generated power and dealing with a lot of mechanical stress arising from various sources. At the same time its shape determines how the rider's body will be positioned in relation to the three points of contact—the pedals, the handlebars, and the saddle.

As I said, more is known about the structure and significance of the main triangle that any other part of the machine, but it is *such* a simple structure that there are few if any deviations from accepted norms in the designing and building of them. Once the bike is on the drawing board, the builder will begin construction by choosing the type of tubing most suited to meeting the stresses that the machine will be subjected to. Some choice also exists in the selection of lugs and bottom bracket shells. Overall the variability of construction details is limited to the following: lug shaping (which includes filing and the possibility of decorative contours or cutouts), bottom-bracket design, design of the seat lug and the method of securing the seat post, the manner of attaching the seat stays, and, finally, the addition of custom "braze-on" fittings such as cable stops, water bottle and derailleur shift lever "bosses," and the like.

The *real* art of building the main triangle, as with the fork, lies in carrying out each operation with care and thoroughness. The tubes must be accurately mitered. That is, the ends that butt against other tube members must be contoured precisely to fit against them without gaps. All "mating" surfaces must be thoroughly cleaned and polished. The lugs must fit over the tube ends with the correct tolerance in order for the braze to flow into the joint properly. Finally, and most importantly, the brazing must be done with the minimum amount of heat necessary to do the job.

THE REAR TRIANGLE

The rather delicate-looking structure made up of the seat stays and the chain stays actually has a surprisingly significant role in determining how a bicycle behaves. First of all the very fact that it is a divided structure—it consists, after all, of *two* triangles that diverge spatially—accounts for a good deal of the frame's "lateral torsional rigidity" (its ability to resist the side-to-side sway induced by strong pedaling). Their spatial configuration—the fact that the chain stays attach toward the outside edges of the bottom bracket and that the triangles spread outward from there—provides a bit of "lateral triangulation," and every little bit helps. The *amount* of divergence or spread is determined by the width of the rear hub and that in turn is often determined by the number of sprockets in the freewheel cluster.

Second, the length of the chain stays is an important factor in determining both the ride and the performance of the bike. The shorter the chain stays, the choppier the ride; but, at the same time, the bicycle becomes easier to accelerate and better at climbing hills. The longer the chain stays (within limits), the more stable and comfortable the ride. The factor that has limited experimentation with chain-stay length on the *short* end of the spectrum has been the diameter of the rear wheel. At a certain point, if the stay gets any shorter, the wheel bumps into the seat tube. Even if you stop short of that point there is still the problem of getting the wheel on and off the bike. Short-wheelbase bikes like sprint and pursuit racers use a dropout with a vertical slot unlike the typical road bike dropout in which the slot slopes forward. Even using a vertical dropout, however, some radical bike designs have required the rear tire to be deflated before the wheel can be installed or removed.

Campagnolo road racing dropout with some detailing added by the builder (Richard Sachs). Note adjustment screws for precise location of the hub axle's position in the dropout.

The shape and size of the seat stays and chain stays aren't terribly significant, at least judging from the variety of sizes in use. Fads seem to dictate lighter stays in some years, heftier stays in others. One would think that systematic engineering analysis would have long since worked out optimal strength-to-weight ratios for these members, but if it has been done, building practice certainly doesn't reflect that.

The chain stays and seat stays meet, of course, at the rear dropouts to which they are brazed. Dropouts, like front-fork tips, are supplied by a number of manufacturers, either forged or cast, but there are more different forms of the rear dropout. The standard road dropout, modeled on the Campagnolo pattern, has a downward and foreward sloping axle slot with screw adjustment of the axle position. The right-hand side dropout has a "boss" or attachment point for the rear derailleur. Another pattern, typical of the Japanese manufacturers, uses a much more sharply downward axle slot. Track dropouts, as mentioned, tend to have a completely vertical slot. They are usually forged and machined.

The manner of fastening the seat stays

Two types of seat stay attachments: (left) the more common method, finished with "biconcave" fluting; (right) the contro- versial "fastback" style devised by Cino Cinelli in which the seat post binder as- sembly is integral with the seat stays.

to the seat lug is one of the minute details by which means builders put their trademarks on their work. To a minimal extent this detail affects the weight and the aerodynamic per- formance of the bike—a *very* minimal extent. The most common method is to braze the stays to the side of the lug and finish them in some interesting way, such as brazing on a fluted "fillet" over the slant-cut end of the stay. The so-called wraparound stay continues the line of the tapered stay up over the top of the seat lug; the two stays are actually joined by a nicely shaped strip of metal. The third principal method of joining seat stays is called

the fastback style. Fastback stays join *behind* the seat lug, usually in conjunction with the binder bolt that holds the seat post in place. The fastback seat stay arrangement was dreamed up allegedly for aerodynamic rea- sons. Many builders criticize it for reducing the strength of the rear triangle. The contro- versy is by no means settled yet. It is not easy to distinguish good frame-building practices— that is, the work of different frame builders from one another. But it is by means of little touches, such as the manner of finishing the seat stays, the shaping and cutting of lugs, and so on, that builders "sign" their work.

Lugwork can be personalized and made decorative in several ways: fancy shaping, cutouts, makers' logos and devices, and special finishing highlights. Small details in bottom bracket treatment also act as makers' signatures (and reduce weight as well).

The serious cyclist lavishes much attention on the components of his or her bicycle. This is natural. They are the things we touch when we ride, the things that move. Many are beautifully made and are therefore pleasing to look at and to touch. It is always a pleasure to use something that *really works*. It is like owning and appreciating fine tools of any sort.

HIGH-TECH COMPONENTS

There is much to say about components. There are many of them in comparison to the frame elements, and each component has undergone its own, independent evolution—as the object of periodic design attention or, in some cases, almost continuous scrutiny over the course of nearly a century.

I do not propose to say all there is to say about bicycle components. My intention here is to describe and examine (and occasion-ally to compare and judge) the components that have become the standards among users and appreciators of fine bicycles. Included will be consideration of recent attempts to change and improve. A few truly new and exotic de-velopments will be reserved for a later chapter.

Let's complete the anatomy lesson we began with the frame. Starting over again at the front of the machine, we will now con-sider the various elements that attach to the

THE NAMING OF PARTS, II

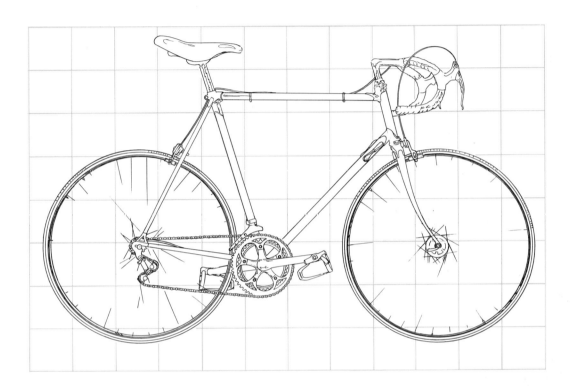

frame and make it into a bicycle.

The front wheel consists of a **tire** seated on a **rim.** In the center of the wheel, suspended by wire **spokes,** is the **hub,** which rotates around the **axle.**

Attached to the steering tube (within the head tube) is the **handlebar stem,** or simply **stem,** which supports the **handlebars.** Mounted on the outward curve of the handlebars (on most bicycles) are the **brake housings** and **brake levers. Brake cables** transmit the mechanical action of the levers to the **brake arms** or **calipers** which force the rubber **brake blocks** or **pads** against the wheel rims to slow or stop the bicycle. (Some specimens—track racing bikes—have no brakes at all.)

Sitting atop the seat tube, supported by the **seat post** is the **seat** or **saddle.**

The drivetrain, the complex of parts that causes the bicycle to move, centers around the **cranks** or **crank arms** which carry the **pedals** on their outer ends. Pedals on high-quality bikes are invariably equipped with **toe clips** and **toe straps** that hold the foot in place to facilitate pedaling. On the inside end the cranks are joined together by the **crank axle** (invisible under normal operating conditions). Attached to the right-hand crank arm are the front driving cogs called the **chain wheels.** (Actually, track bikes have only one; others have two or three.)

The **chain** (a system made up of inner and outer link plates fastened by steel pins encircled by rollers) transmits the motion of the chain wheel to the rear wheel of the bicycle. The rear driving cogs, called the **rear cluster** or the **freewheel cogs,** are mounted on a special part of the rear hub and axle assembly called the **freewheel.** The freewheel is a ratchet mechanism that causes the wheel to rotate forward when pulled by the chain and allows it to continue rotating even when the chain stops moving. Track bikes have only one rear cog and no freewheel. The freewheel and multiple driving cogs are the only features that make the rear wheel different from the front.

Finally, for bicycles other than track bikes, there is a gear-shifting system. Mounted on the down tube (usually) are a pair of **gearshift levers.** They manipulate cables that operate the front and rear **derailleurs,** the French name for the gear-shifting mechanisms that move the chain from one driving cog to another.

THE WHEEL AND WHEEL BUILDING

The wheel was, of course, the point of departure for the bicycle; the inspiration and the *sine qua non.* A fine bicycle wheel has a simple beauty—it is a pretty amazing piece of engineering, once you stop to think about it.

The wheel had been in use for several thousand years by the time even the most primitive precursor of the modern cycle appeared on the scene, and the earliest mid-nineteenth-century bicycle wheels were the products of carriage builders. Within the first thirty years of frenetic bicycle development, however, great strides were made in the technology of wheel building and, in a very real sense, each owes much to the other.

One of the earliest significant improvements over the technology of the carriage wheel was the invention of a better method of easing the bearing surfaces of the hubs and axles. Other things were tried, but it was the ball-bearing system that created the first revolution in wheel building in the early 1870s. Ball bearings were first used on some of the earlier sophisticated high-wheeled ordinaries of that period.

Within a year or two of the introduction of ball bearings came the transition from the carriage builder's system of using rigid spokes—each capable of bearing the full weight of bicycle and rider in direct compression—to the so-called suspension system of spoking in which light, ductile wires held the hub suspended at the geometric center of the rim, exerting equal and opposite forces on one another. The first suspended wheels used radial spokes—going from the hub to the rim by the shortest possible route—but almost immediately after the introduction of the suspension principle came the variation known as tangent spoking, in which the spoke left the hub at a tangent, thus increasing its capacity to absorb shock and stress and improving its efficiency at transmitting rotation.

With the advent of the chain-driven safety bicycle in the mid-1880s the front-wheel spindle stopped being a part of the crank mechanism, and the configuration of hubs and axles rapidly evolved that is still standard today. The axles of both wheels became immovable, fixed to the forks while the hubs rotated around them. The system consisted of bearing "races" fixed to the inside of the hub and "cones" threaded onto the ends of the axle or spindle. The balls ran in the space between the cones and the races, the fit of the parts being adjustable by means of screwing the cones in or out, increasing or decreasing the overall spacing and, hence, tightness. Locknuts threaded on the outboard side of the cones prevented them from changing position—getting out of adjustment. All of the bearing parts—the cones, the races, and the balls—were made of fine steel and were made even more durable by the heat treatment known as case hardening.

It was and remains a very efficient system. The ball-bearing hub-and-axle articulation, given proper lubrication and adjustment, provides as strong and as frictionless a connection between the moving and non-moving parts of the wheel as anyone has yet devised.

Many of the early velocipede wheels were made from wood (again, carrying on the traditional practices of carriage building), but with the invention of the tensioned wire spoke, which brought the rim much more into play in terms of the strength of the overall structure, builders quickly discovered that wood wasn't strong enough to do the job. Wooden rims just didn't hold their shape, so makers quickly switched to iron and, later on, to steel.

The early iron or iron-shod wooden wheels made for a pretty punishing ride, as you can imagine, especially considering the state of road-building technology. Though this didn't stop people from cycling, it did lead, fairly early on, to the idea of attaching a padding of rubber to the outside of the rim to provide some cushion—the prototype of the tire. But it took some time for the first true tires to evolve. The first specifically manufactured tires were made for James Starley's Ariel, first produced in 1871. They were composite, spongy on the underside, tougher on the tread. They were more or less round in section.

Seventeen years later the first patent was taken out for a pressurized pneumatic tire—a development that constituted a giant leap for cycling. It made bicycles faster, safer, *and* more comfortable. Within a year or two of its introduction in the marketplace (and the race track) the Dunlop pneumatic tire (and, a bit later, the Michelin) had virtually replaced all other types.

So by about 1895 the bicycle wheel had evolved (through many forms) to something very much like what we know today. From this point on very little development took place in basic wheel-building technology. Most of the changes fall under the category of small refinements, often resulting from improvements in materials—such as using first steel and later aluminum alloys to make lighter rims, or minor changes resulting from engineering changes in gearing systems and the like.

One of the more interesting innovations that did come along was the product of the genius of Tuillo Campagnolo, founder of the famous firm of bicycle-components manu-

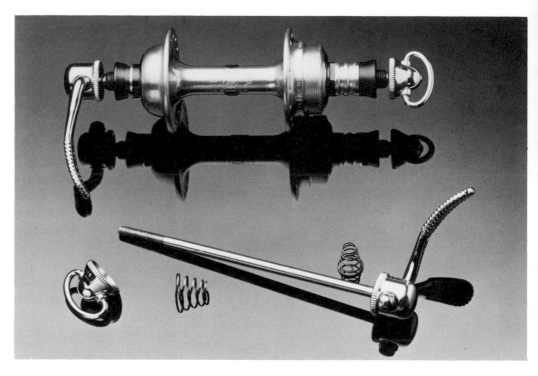

The quick-release hub—one of the early inventions of Tuillo Campagnolo.

facturers. In 1927 Campagnolo, an active bike racer, invented a new way of fastening the wheel to the bicycle—and *unfastening* it. He was motivated in this enterprise by an unfortunate experience. Campagnolo suffered a puncture during a race in particularly nasty winter weather. His fingers were so cold that he could not manage to loosen the wing nuts (also frozen) that held his wheel to the fork. His resolution to come up with a better, foolproof way of attaching and detaching wheels led him to design the "quick-release skewer." Brilliant in its simplicity, there is no way it can fail to work (as long as the materials are reliable). There were two principal or essential ideas combined in this invention. One was the use of the eccentric cam; the other was the use of a hollow axle. A hollow axle, however, if it was to be strong enough, necessitated new steels—steels hard enough to make up for the reduced cross section. Fortunately new steel alloys were being developed at that time, so the invention worked. It has stood the test of time, too, and today is a fea-

ture of virtually every fine road bicycle.

One other significant development was the invention of tubular or "sew-up" tires, in which the outer casing completely surrounded the inner air-holding tube, producing a perfectly round cross section. This type of tire also required a different type of rim; one that provided a round, concave, smooth surface for the tire to bed against. The solution of fastening tire to rim was to glue it on. The entire assembly of tubular tire and rim was much lighter than the "beaded" or "wired-on" tires that came before them. The significance of this development, from an engineering point of view, centers around the fact that getting mass into motion on the outer edge of a wheel requires more expenditure of energy than that required to move the non-rotating parts, weight for weight. (The same holds true for stopping that motion.) In fact it takes roughly *twice* the energy to set the same amount of weight revolving as it does to get it moving in a straight line, so any weight saving here counts roughly double.

MODERN BICYCLE WHEELS

So much for evolution. Let's take a closer look at the modern bicycle wheel and try to get a handle on the options available to the cyclist.

The hub is the logical place to begin (at the center). The basic design is very much the same for all types of carefully made conventional hubs; only some of the details differ. The axle is threaded on both ends, whether it is solid or hollow. (Track-racing bicycles don't use quick-release hubs, therefore they use solid-steel axles for the extra strength.) The precisely machined and polished bearing cones are screwed onto the axle—one on each side. On the typical hollow-axle, quick-release hub, a key slot is cut in the threaded portion of the axle to accommodate a keyed washer that goes just to the outside of the bearing cone. Outboard of the washer is the locknut that keeps the cone from moving from its carefully adjusted position. A typical solid-section track hub axle lacks the keyed washer between the bearing cone and its locknut, but uses instead a knurled lock washer between the locknut and the fork tip or dropout.

The hub housing is forged of light-weight aluminum alloy. The housing bulges outward at either end to accommodate the hardened steel bearing cups or races that are pressed into place there. The balls run freely in the spaces between the cups, which are part of the hub housing, and the cones, which are essentially part of the axle. Proper adjustment of the bearings involves tightening or loosening the cones until there is no feel of binding or rolling resistance, but no suggestion of play or looseness either. Adjustment is made with very thin, flat wrenches especially designed to fit the narrow "flats" on the cones and locknuts. Once the cones are properly adjusted, the locknuts are tightened against them to keep them in place.

The hub flanges, to which the spokes attach, are angled inward slightly, toward the rims, and are generally "pierced" or drilled to reduce weight. Most manufacturers offer a choice of flange height. Typical high-flange hubs have an overall diameter of about 3 inches (75 millimeters). Typical low-flange hubs are slightly under 2 inches in diameter (about 45 millimeters). While the low-flange will make a marginally lighter wheel, the real choice between high-flange and low-flange is a trade-off between strength and comfort.

The high-flange hub makes a stiffer, more rigid wheel for two reasons—one easy to understand, the other a bit more complex. The first is simply that with a high-flange hub, the spokes will be shorter. The less distance between the hub and the rim that is

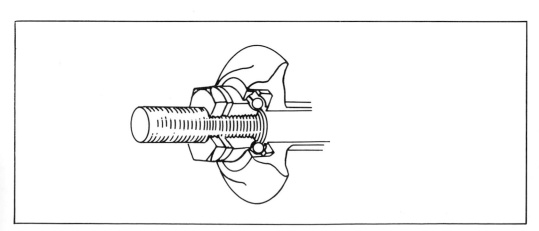

Typical adjustable hub bearing system consisting of balls running between cups in the hub body and adjustable cones threaded onto the spindle and held in place with locknuts.

High-flange track hub from Campagnolo.

taken up by flexible, ductile wire, the more rigid the structure will inevitably be. (Incidently the shorter spokes do make up for some of the extra weight of a high-flange hub.)

The second reason relates specifically to the ability of the wheel to handle sideways stresses (engineers call them lateral loads) such as it is subjected to in cornering—stresses operating in the axis of the wheel axle. It all has to do with the *angles* at which structures do their work of opposing loads. If you have studied any elementary physics, you will already have the conceptual tools to understand this problem; but even if you haven't, it is really not that complicated.

The most efficient configuration for a structure in relation to a force it is opposing is to be in direct opposition to the direction of that force. A good illustration would be for you to tie a 10-pound weight to a short piece of rope. Let your arm hang straight down—in

direct opposition to the load—and you have no trouble supporting it. Now hold your arm straight out in front of you. You will notice that considerably more effort is required to support the weight. With your arm hanging straight down, you might well be able to hold that weight for an hour without discomfort. With your arm outstretched, the chances are you would not be able to hold it for more than half a minute, if that.

So much for the analogy. Your muscles tire and cannot maintain their ability to contract. Metal structures of the kind we are talking about deform or bend in response to stress up to the point at which their ability to oppose the load is surpassed, whereupon they deform permanently or break. The most efficient way for a structure to oppose a load, again, is in direct opposition. The farther away from direct opposition that the load-bearing structure gets—as the load angle decreases from 180° to 90°—the greater the ef-

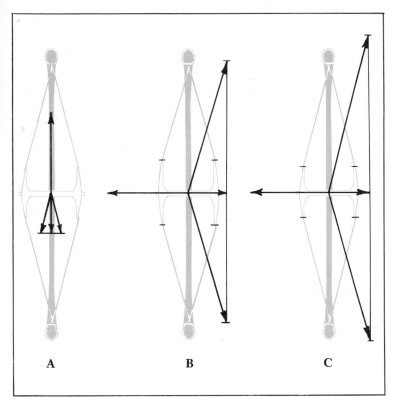

A   B   C

A) Axial loads are handled easily by the suspended wheel structure: upward arrow represents the load; downward arrow (center) represents the force opposing the load divided between the two physical structures (spokes) that do the job.

B) High-flange hub. This diagram shows the effective load borne by spokes when opposing lateral loads. The job, as above, is divided between two spokes, each bearing one-half the load.

C) With low-flange hubs, the more obtuse load angle means greater lateral load effect; i.e. spokes are subjected to greater effective loads or, conversely, are deflected more for a given lateral load, compared with high-flange hubs.

fective load becomes, or, to put it another way, the less efficient the structure becomes in opposing that load. As the load angle approaches 90° the effective load approaches infinity (or the load-bearing efficiency drops toward zero) regardless of the magnitude of the actual load.

So now picture the bicycle wheel. It is quite efficient in opposing up-and-down loads, those that run from rim to rim. The spokes are reasonably close to being in direct opposition to such loads. But it is also reasonably easy to see that they are *not* in a very good position to resist lateral loads. In fact they are getting dangerously close to the 90° relationship at which, theoretically, they would be unable to oppose them at all. (In this somewhat simplified analysis the theory relates to "perfectly elastic" structures that oppose loads entirely by means of their tensile strength. Fortunately steel has other properties that help out.) It is simply that the

greater the angle of the apex of the triangle that the spokes form coming from the flanges to the center of the rim, the more efficient they are at opposing lateral loads. As the illustrations make clear (in a slightly exaggerated way), a high-flange hub makes a triangle with a wider angle than does a low-flange hub; thus a high-flange wheel will deform less in response to a given lateral load than will a low-flange hub, all other things being equal.

So why use low-flange hubs at all? One simple answer. The low-flange hub, with its longer spokes, gives a more cushioned ride. (It is less efficient than the high-flange at opposing up-and-down loads too!) A sacrifice in the mechanical efficiency of the structure is more than made up for in the beneficial effect on the rider, who is not worn out from the physical punishment of rough riding surfaces. The classic situation is that of the European cobblestone roads over which many of the important road races are run. The *pavé*, as it is known, is an invention of the devil as far as the cyclist is concerned, and any relief from the continual pounding the rider receives is a mercy. Hence low-flange hubs.

The only other reason for using a low-flange hub would be for the minimal weight saving that might be crucial for a racer preparing or attempting to break a time-trial record. In such a case it would probably be combined with radial spoking—another unusual, if not radical, measure these days.

This brings us to one of the more hotly debated aspects of wheel building: spokes and spoking patterns. There is less controversy about the former than the latter, but we'll

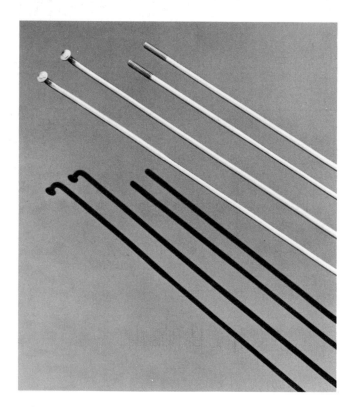

Plain-gauge and butted spokes. The differences are subtle (the butted spokes are the lower members of each pair) and easier to see in the reflection.

take a quick look anyway. Spokes are available in either butted form (thicker at the ends, thinner in the middle) or plain gauge. They are also available in two different types of steel: stainless steel or ordinary "mild" steel, either galvanized or chrome plated. Both the butted and the stainless options would appear to be more "high-tech," but a lot of serious wheel builders stay away from both. Butted spokes, they say, are less stiff. This causes increased vibration or "whip" over the whole length of the spoke, putting more stress on the most vulnerable points—the ends—and resulting in more broken spokes. Detractors of stainless spokes, though they usually acknowledge their attractive appearance and resistance to corrosion, point out that the stainless steels used in spoke manufacture have about 25 percent less tensile strength than mild steel.

The subject of spoking patterns can arouse true passion among serious wheel builders. Adherents of several different systems all seem to hold their views with equal conviction. There is something slightly mystical about it.

Theoretically there are five possible arrangements of spokes in relation to the hub and to the other spokes, distinguished from one another in terms of the number of times any given spoke crosses another. These run from radial spoking in which there is no spoke crossing to "four-cross," in which each spoke, naturally, makes four crossings. The vast majority of bicycle wheels are spoked in the three-cross pattern. Radial spoking *is* used, but rarely. It is an extreme practice, designed to save weight at all costs. It cannot be used on a rear wheel at all, due to its minimal ability to resist "hub windup." I don't know of a single instance in which one-cross spoking has been used, although I'm sure it has at one time or another. Similarly two-cross is not used very often. I guess it is mostly a case of an inadequate trade-off.

Brothers Italo and Paolo Guerciotti, both former racers and team mechanics, joined forces with their uncle, Lino Tempesta, an experienced artisan, and began building frames in the mid-1960s. With a little help along the way from Cino Cinelli, the Guerciotti frame has gained a very wide following both in Europe and the U. S. The Guerciottis build road racing frames only.

Colnago and Masi are two more of the world's most highly revered frame builders. Both work in Milan, along with a good number of the rest: Cinelli, Pogliaghi, DeRosa, Guerciotti, etc. Colnago's bikes have achieved wide recognition in the last ten years or so, being used by a number of national teams and professional racers.

The Masi is probably the single most sought-after bicycle in the world. Masi's production is almost totally monopolised by professional European racing teams. The family firm is now in its second generation, making it one of the oldest, if not the oldest, in the business. Masi is one of the very few Italian builders who chooses Reynolds tubing.

The '3 Rensho' is an unusual product in a land where mass production is the norm. The bike is produced by builder Yoshi Konno in a relatively small, personally supervised handwork operation, turning out fewer than 1,000 frames per year. The 'Rensho' utilizes Japanese materials and components and features a number of unusual design details, such as brake and derailleur cables running inside frame tubes.

American frame builders are beginning to gain some significant recognition—especially among American riders. One of the most respected of the recently emerging Americans is Richard Sachs. Sachs makes only one bicycle: the 'Signature' frame set, available by itself or as a built-up bike featuring either a Nuovo Record or a Super Record component "group." Sachs frames feature Colombus tubes, Cinelli bottom bracket shells, and impeccable workmanship and finish.

S aavedra, an Argentinian builder better known in Europe than in the States, has been turning out fine handmade bicycle frames for over thirty years—part of that time in Italy. This Saavedra track bike is set up with the new, miniaturized "10-pitch" drive components from Shimano.

This is a no-non-sense racing frame from Rossin, relative newcomer to the Italian cycle building world. Clean workmanship and a few up-to-date touches like the aerodynamic fork crown separate the Rossin frame from the run of the mill.

Three styles of hub from Campagnolo. The high-flange hub makes the strongest wheel. The low flange is a compromise designed to reduce the transmission of road shock through the wheels. The design of the "hi-lo" hub is aimed at equalizing the spoke stresses in "dished" rear wheels of road racing and touring bikes.

Shimano's Dura-Ace AX brake arch and lever. Squeezing the lever causes the triangular cam to move upward, forcing the upper ends of the calipers outward, which in turn brings the pads against the wheel rim. With this system, relatively small lever motion generates relatively great caliper motion—and considerable mechanical advantage.

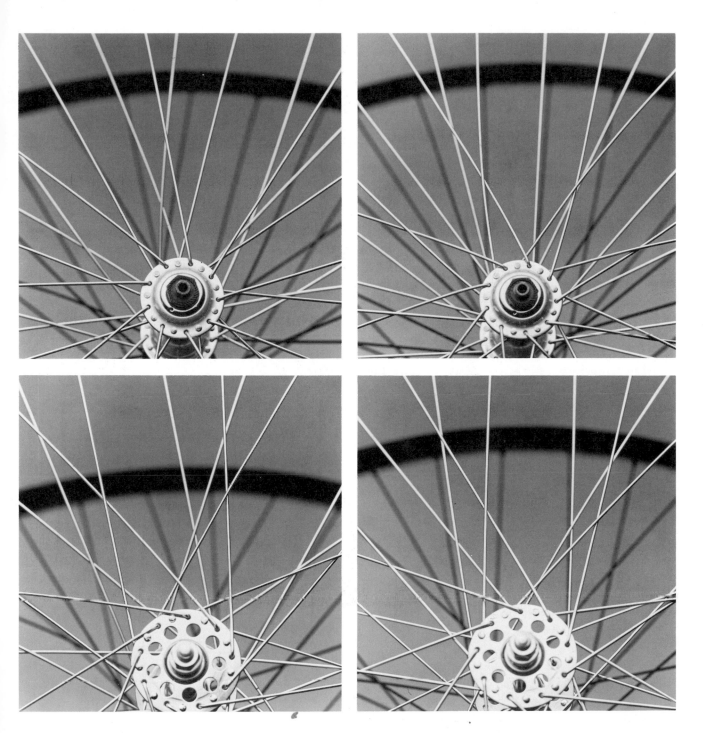

F our of the five possible wheel-lacing patterns (clockwise, beginning top left): one-, two-, three-, and four-cross wheels.

The hottest debate is between the advocates of three-cross and four-cross wheel building. I mentioned that the majority of wheels are built three-cross, but among professional wheel builders opinion is equally divided (in other words, the three-cross wheel is an "original-equipment manufacturer's" standard). Those who take up the cudgels for four-cross wheels argue that a well-built one is virtually indestructible, and they cite numerous convincing stories to support their positions, such as crashes in which rims and forks were destroyed but not a spoke was broken. For what it is worth, I have *never* broken a spoke on my twenty-year-old road-racing bike's four-cross wheels.

The counterargument of the three-cross advocates is that this is overkill; that a well-built three-cross wheel is adequate to any normal cycling test (emphasis on well-built and on normal). There can be little argument that the three-cross wheel is lighter.

There is also a less rigid group of wheel-building mavens who wisely counsel that the ideal spoking for *your* bicycle depends on whatever use you intend to put it. A heavily loaded touring bike is going to need a heftier wheel than one that's just going to be pedaled around Central Park.

But there is more to spoking patterns than the ability of the wheel to stand up to punishment. It also affects the efficiency of the transfer of torque (rotation) from the hub to the rim. The more crosses in the spoking pattern, the more nearly tangential is the path of the spoke in relation to the hub. The more nearly tangential the spoke, the more efficient it is in transmitting the torque. The spoke of a four-cross wheel is *truly* at a tangent to the hub and as such has maximum efficiency; it is pulling in a straight line at a point on the rim that is, rotationally speaking, directly behind it—another case of a structure relating to a load in direct opposition. In less truly tangential orientation there is always some

tendency for the spokes to bend under acceleration, resulting in the phenomenon known as hub windup, in which the rear hub "gets ahead of" the rim.

Further wheel building arguments revolve around questions of the relative efficiency of spokes that run from the outside of the flange as opposed to the inside, symmetrical versus asymmetrical wheels. (The former are wheels whose corresponding spokes on opposite flanges are laced in mirror image—i.e., from inside to outside or vice versa—or have the same orientation—i.e., from left to right or vice versa.) As I said, these are areas of controversy. There doesn't seem to be very general agreement on these questions, and at times it seems very much as if the arguments get into the realm of the mystical.

DISHED WHEELS

One very real and practical problem occurs in connection with the rear wheels of multiple-geared bicycles. The gear sprockets that make up the freewheel cluster take up quite a bit of space on the right-hand side of the wheel axle. The wheel rim must, of course, still be centered between the two ends of the axle. The solution to the problem of fitting all of these elements together is to "dish" the wheel—tighten the spokes on the freewheel side to the point that they make a much steeper angle with respect to the wheel axle than the spokes on the left-hand side. Accordingly the right-hand hub flange is much closer to the center of the axle than the left-hand flange. This all adds up to a situation in which the structure is significantly "out of balance." The spokes on the freewheel side are under much greater tension to begin with and, due to their steeper angle, their capacity to oppose lateral loads is significantly reduced. Thus, when any lateral load is applied to the wheel, these spokes will be stressed

Three rear road racing hubs from Campagnolo. The "hi-lo" hub (center) is designed to help equalize spoke tensions in dished rear wheels by allowing the spokes of the freewheel side to assume more or less the same load angles as the opposing spokes.

much more heavily than those on the opposite side. They are operating continuously at a stress level considerably closer to their breaking strength than the other spokes.

For a long time the side effects of wheel dishing were just something that the cyclist had to live with, but some recent engineering developments have gone part of the way in dealing with these problems. The first of these is a relatively simple development—a rear hub with a higher flange on the freewheel side than on the left-hand side. The so-called hi-lo hub provides two related benefits or improvements. It gives the freewheel-side spokes

a more favorable load-resisting angle and significantly reduces the spoke tension on the freewheel side necessary to reconcile the off-center hub with the centered rim.

The Shimano Company also attacked the problem of wheel dishing and recently came up with a somewhat more complex solution, resulting in several interesting changes in the structure of the rear hub. One element of Shimano's "Uni-balance" hub that differs significantly from the conventional is the freewheel-side bearing, which is normally *inboard* of the freewheel and thus much closer to the center of the axle than the left-hand

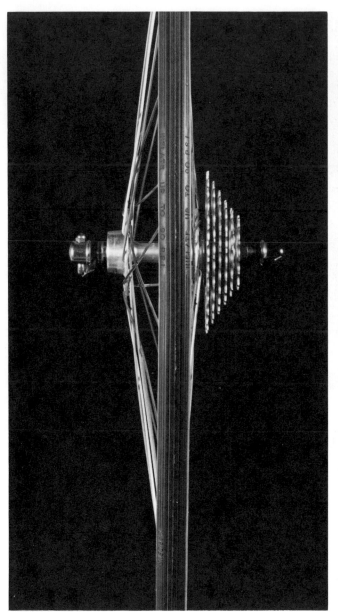 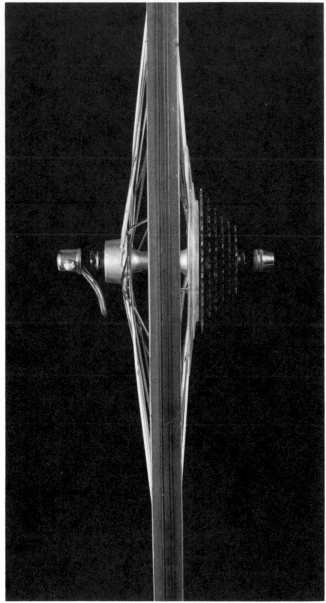

F reewheel-side spokes in a conventional dished wheel are almost straight up and down and are at a markedly different angle than opposite spokes, meaning that they are at much higher tension.

S himano's 'Uni Balance' hub design allows the wheel axis to much more closely approximate the midpoint between the flanges, equalizing spoke angles and tension significantly.

The 'Uni Balance' hub design also moves the freewheel-side bearing to the outboard end of the axle, inside the 'Cassette' body.

bearing. On the Uni-balance hub, the freewheel-side bearing has been moved much farther outward and the left-hand bearing brought in slightly so that the two bearings are now symmetrical with respect to the rim. This cannot help but have a beneficial effect on overall load distribution.

This meant, however, that the wheel bearing and the freewheel mechanism were now occupying the same space. What the Shimano engineers did was to build the freewheel *around* the bearing. This helped further by making room to move the freewheel-side flange somewhat farther to the outside. Combine this with moving the left-hand flange *in* slightly and you have a much more structurally balanced wheel (although it is not by any means totally balanced). Shimano figures claim reduction of the total wheel dishing imbalance to about one-third of that typical of conventional rear wheels and cite greatly reduced vibration in the total wheel assembly as a result.

A more general attempt to improve the

A Phil Wood hub compared to a typical "Italian-style" hub. The former features medium height flanges, a larger diameter hub body for more efficient torque transfer, and sealed bearing assemblies.

bicycle wheel hub came from American inventor Phil Wood in the mid 1970s. Wood's hubs are more ruggedly engineered than the traditional "Italian-style" hubs. They employ both a larger diameter axle and a larger diameter hub housing, improving both overall strength and torque transmission efficiency. Wood's hubs also replaced the traditional cup-and-cone bearing with sealed, precision ball-bearing assemblies, improving bearing efficiency a bit and reducing or virtually eliminating maintenance. Hubs similar in overall engineering and style are manufactured by the Hi-E Corporation and other American firms. The sealed-bearing idea particularly has caught on with a number of manufacturers and sealed-bearing hubs are becoming more and more widely available, although they are substantially more costly than conventional hubs.

TIRES AND RIMS

Tires

These two tires have similar treads and intended uses. The inside tire is of tubular or "sew-up" construction and costs several times more than the wired-on. Although wired-on tires have improved dramatically in recent years, top performance requirements still dictate the use of tubulars.

For a long time there have been two different types of bicycle tires available: the wired-on type (popularly known as the clincher tire) and the tubular or "sew-up." The wired-on tire has been of very little interest to the serious cyclist, with the exception of those who tour with heavy loads over rough roads—until very recently, that is. Sew-ups have always been *so* much lighter and more responsive. Sew-up tires are the thoroughbreds; wired-ons, the workhorses.

The less expensive types of sew-ups (still more costly than the finest wired-ons) are made by vulcanizing a tread onto a cotton casing or sidewall. This is a mechanized process in most cases. The better tubular tires, however, are made by gluing the tread to the casing *by hand*, without the use of heat. This produces a more resilient tire. The casings of handmade ("cold process") tubulars are either of fine cotton or, in the best and lightest models, of silk. The cotton casing is more durable—or, to put it the other way around, less vulnerable to abuse—but given proper care, silk tires provide the ultimate in light weight and responsiveness.

Again, the less expensive sew-up tires use a Butyl inner tube, similar to the familiar tubes for wired-ons but lighter. The finer tires use a tube of natural latex which is not only lighter, but more resistant to punctures. (The latex tube is more *elastic* than the Butyl, making it more likely that the tube will yield to an object that penetrates the tread rather than being penetrated in turn.) The trade-off with latex tubes is that they don't hold pressure very effectively. A Butyl tube pumped up to optimum pressure will maintain *acceptable* pressure for better than two weeks, whereas a latex tube will fall below acceptable pressure levels within twelve hours. The lightest silk-latex sew-up tires, made for racing on smooth board tracks, weigh a scant 185 grams (just a bit more than 6½ ounces).

As recently as ten years ago many midline production bicycles came with sew-up tires as standard equipment. Nowadays only the top-of-the-line bicycle comes so equipped. Why the change? Well, part of the answer is economic. Sew-up tires are costly, the most expensive being between three and four times the price of the costliest wired-ons, largely due to greater labor costs in their manufacture. Demand has also outstripped supply, driving the cost up further. Then there is the fact that sew-ups require a *lot* of TLC. Repairing them is a hassle. They must be removed from the rim—unglued—carefully unstitched along the casing seam (in the right place), patched, restitched, and remounted on the rim—a lot of work. For greatest puncture resistance they must be bought long before the date of intended use and aged, stretched on spare rims, so that the tread material hardens. Tubular tires are often aged for up to a year or

more before being put into use. Meanwhile their sidewalls will deteriorate if they are not stored in a cool, dark, dry place and coated with a special protective latex solution—and so on. Performance certainly has its price.

Meanwhile, over the past decade, an expanding bicycle industry desperately needed to find a way to provide higher-performance tires to an ever-increasing market at a cost that people could afford and in quantities that would meet the growing demand. Now wired-on tires have always offered certain advantages—primarily low cost, relative ease of repair, and greater ruggedness. Over the past decade experimentation with new materials—such as nylon sidewall fabrics and new synthetic fibers like the incredibly strong Kevlar—and with new tread-bonding techniques, combined with some systematic research into efficient tread designs, has resulted in a revolution in the quality of the wired-on. Wired-ons can now be obtained in weights equivalent to the lightest and finest sew-ups, operating at similar inflation pressures and at a fraction of the cost (which reduces inflation*ary* pressures considerable). In short, wired-on tires have become a much more viable option for the serious bicyclist.

Rims

The proverbial albatross of the new, lightweight wired-on tire is the rim. Rims for wired-on tires are more complex in cross section than rims for tubulars, so they require a heavier extrusion. All high-quality rims are made from light aluminum alloys (as opposed to steel) with rims for sew-ups ranging in weight between 250 and 350 grams (8.8 and 12.3 ounces) each. The weight range for good wired-on rims is roughly 475 to 500 grams (16.75 to 17.6 ounces)—a much smaller range, but also a much greater weight. This represents the most significant advantage that tubular tires still have over wired-ons. On average the rim will weigh at least 200 grams (about 7 ounces or nearly half a pound) more and, as the rule of thumb tells us, weight differences in rolling parts are effectively doubled. So until a way is found to bring down the weight of rims for wired-ons, they will always have an inherent disadvantage in terms of responsiveness and acceleration.

In general, as mentioned, high-quality bicycle rims are made from lightweight aluminum alloys, and have been for some time. Unless they are being built for minimum possible weight, all alloy rims are ferruled. That is, a small reinforcing grommet is attached to each spoke hole. For ultra-lightweight rims the grommet is replaced by a small washer that supports the spoke nipple, making the total rim marginally lighter. Among the few technical innovations to come along in the rim-building trade recently has been the development of super-strong lightweight rims, made by elaborate heat treatment of special alloys—making for a rim that stands up to practically any punishment that a cyclist can dish out (without crashing)—at about five times the cost of standard, high-quality rims.

THE POINTS OF CONTACT

THE PEDAL

The pedal is another of those elements essential to the concept of the bicycle as we know it. The essence of Michaux's invention was the attachment of pedals to a set of crank arms. The crank, after all, had been around for a long time, used for various purposes—turning grindstones, for example—but the pedal, a secure platform for the feet to do the work (as opposed to the hands), originated with the bicycle. It is a familiar element. We tend to take it for granted. So did cyclists and cycle designers throughout most of the history of the bicycle. The basic design of the bicycle pedal has not changed significantly since well before the turn of the century—not, that is, until fairly recently.

In the early days pedals went through a lot of forms. This was partly due to the riding technique of "pre-freewheel" bicycles. With fixed cranks, the rider had to take the feet off of the pedals when coasting down hills, so it was important to make it easy for the rider to find a new purchase after the downhill run was over. In exploring this problem early designers came up with square, blocklike pedals, triangular pedals, and even round pedals, settling finally on the flat "rattrap" design.

The rattrap pedal became the standard after the invention of the freewheel. It was no longer necessary to facilitate the rider's getting his or her foot back onto the pedal surface, as there was no longer any reason to remove the foot. The flat pedal with a central, housed axle or spindle with a square strip of rubber, felt, or other material on either side served the purpose and was relatively light in weight. The toe clip, that invaluable aid to efficient pedaling, was invented and added to the basic rattrap design well before the turn of the century.

The only changes in pedal design over the next fifty to sixty years were of the refinement variety, not of fundamental innovation. The rattrap was made lighter and stronger. Specific modifications evolved for different types of riding. The outside rubber strips were soon replaced by a metal cage that supported the foot in much the same way—first of steel, later, of light aluminum alloys. Quite significant for performance was the invention of the shoe cleat, which engaged the rear edge of the pedal cage and helped to keep the rider's foot in place.

A modern, refined rattrap or "cage" pedal consists of the followig elements: a steel axle or spindle, threaded on the inboard end to attach to the crank arm and incorporating an integral bearing cone, also on the inboard end; a light alloy housing or body that surrounds the spindle and contains the bearing races and to which the cage is fastened; and an adjustable bearing cone threaded onto the outboard end of the spindle, secured by a locknut, and protected from dirt and moisture by a cap nut.

Again the spindle is of hardened steel, to withstand the considerable forces of strong pedaling. The cones, races, and ball bearings are precisely ground and polished to reduce friction. The remaining parts of the pedal, the body, the cage, and the cap nut are of light alloy. This then is a typical, high-quality, conventional pedal.

It seems odd, since in the early days the pedal took so many forms—round, four-sided, three-sided, and, ultimately, two sided—that it didn't seem to occur to anyone (for a long time) that for the rider who used a toe clip and strap, the pedal had become in effect a one-sided form.

The first pedal design that recognized this fact explicitly and sought to capitalize on it was the work of the Frenchman Marcel Berthet. The Berthet "platform" pedal offered more support to the foot than the conventional cage, distributing force more evenly while offering just as secure an attachment. One of the benefits was increased clearance.

Another platform pedal was developed by the Italian designer and frame-builder Cino Cinelli. Cinelli's pedal is an even more radical departure from the conventional; even the toe clip and strap are eliminated. The rider's foot is held in place by a special cleat that attaches to the bottom of the shoe and locks into place on the pedal by means of a sliding lever. The difficulty of engaging and disengaging the lock mechanism makes this pedal impractical for any but the track racer (you certainly couldn't ride with it in traffic), but it is a very effective design, again, in increasing clearance, and reducing weight and air drag.

Two very recent entries into the field are updated, reengineered versions of the platform pedal concept introduced by the U.S. firm, Avocet, and the Japanese firm, Shimano.

The Avocet Model III platform pedal streamlines the basic platform shape by tapering where a shoe tapers. Good support is provided for the front portion of the foot and a ridge at the rear of the platform engages the shoe cleat, just as with a cage pedal. Presumably for weight-saving purposes as well as ease of manufacture, the body of the pedal is molded from a "durable, lightweight, fiber-loaded composite." Part of the new design is a toe clip somewhat simpler, presumably stronger and marginally lighter than the conventional. Whereas the standard toe clip is designed to attach to the *front* of the cage (and makes a 90° bend in order to do so), it cannot be adjusted in length. The clip on the Avocet Model III *is* adjustable forward and back—and side to side.

Shimano's "DD" pedal, although similar to the Avocet in some respects, is an even more radical departure. Like the Avocet it is more rigorously designed from an aerodynamic standpoint (in fact that is Shimano's big marketing point at the moment). It also has a

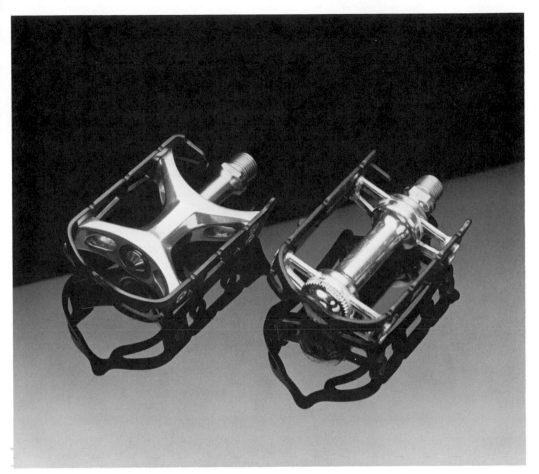

The Campagnolo Record road pedal (right) and an up-to-date, lightweight descendant, the Sun Tour 'Pro Superbe.'

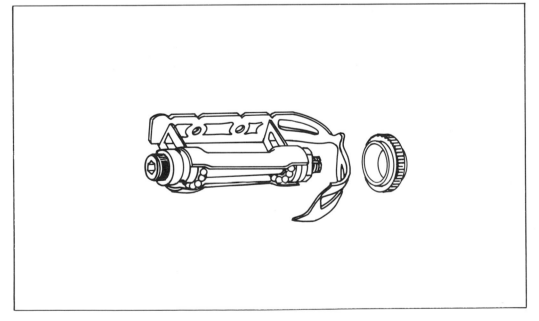

Cutaway drawing of a typical cage pedal shows cups, balls, and cones supporting the pedal body around the spindle. Dust cap (right) screws over the end of the assembly to keep things clean.

very similar toe clip system, but here the similarities end. Much more interesting and promising is a major engineering alteration.

All cycling engineers and theorists seem to agree that the proper orientation of the foot to the pedal is with the ball of the foot directly over the pedal axle. All previous designs have indeed placed it there—over, but also *above* the pedal axle. This means that while the axle describes one circle as the crank spins, the ball of the foot describes another circle, slightly displaced spatially. Shi-

mano's engineers contend that some of the rider's pedaling energy is dissipated in maintaining pedal stability as a result of this discrepancy. This is a subtle and sophisticated engineering argument, but it does have a certain intuitive appeal to me (as a layman)—it *sounds* reasonable. Anyway, the Shimano engineers set about to reconcile the two centers, so to speak. The solution they came up with was to *eliminate* the pedal axle, at least that portion that has passed under the rider's foot in all previous designs. The result is that the

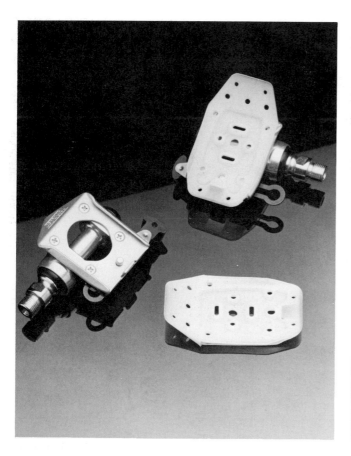

The Cinelli platform pedal: massive bearings and minimal foot support. The cleat locks the rider's foot to the pedal surface.

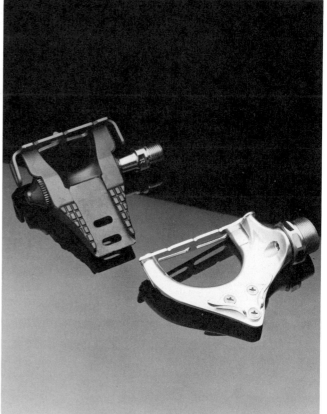

The aerodynamic Avocet Model III pedal (left) is molded from lightweight plastic. The Shimano 'D D' pedal is the first to eliminate the spindle which ordinarily runs through the pedal body underneath the foot. Note the oversized bearing where the pedal attaches to the crank.

pedal *axis* now, in effect, passes through the rider's foot. Again, intuitively, this seems as if it should result in improved pedaling action.

If nothing else, however, it increases the effective length of the crank arm without affecting clearance; or, to put it the other way around, this design should give significantly better pedal clearance for the same crank length and bottom bracket height. In other words it should make it possible to build a bicycle with its center of gravity half an inch lower to the ground without sacrificing clear-ance; no small achievement. Critics are quick to point out that the design has yet to be test-ed by time and the punishment meted out by racing cyclists. It seems clear that the de-mands placed on the pedal body and the sin-gle bearing will be great. Time will tell, and improvements will undoubtedly be made.

Meanwhile, what kind of pedals *do* racers use? The most carefully thought-out and carefully manufactured and finished ver-sion of the conventional rattrap: the Cam-pagnolo pedal. Racers are a conservative lot.

Another sealed-bearing pedal. On the Assos pedal, the spindle reaches only halfway out the width of the pedal body, giving better clearance than con-ventional pedals.

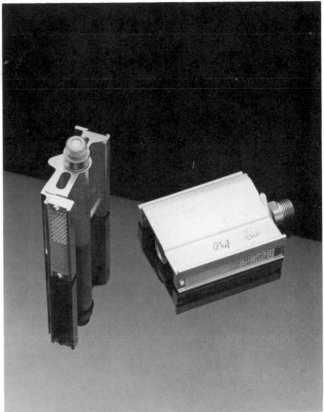

The Phil Wood ped-al, another new-comer to the scene. Note integral fore-and-aft reflectors. Pread-justed sealed bearings are part of the Phil Wood tradition.

HANDLEBARS

The subject of handlebars is not a vast one, and not much in the way of high technology is involved. Not much has changed in the last forty years or so. Still, they're part of the package, so let's have a look.

Bicycle handlebars attach to the frame by means of an angled fitting known as the **handlebar stem,** or just the **stem,** that fits inside the steering tube. The dimensions of the stem determine the position of the handlebars, both fore-and-aft and vertically. Stems are available in a variety of "extension" lengths. The rider chooses a stem that throws the bars the appropriate distance forward of the steering head to suit the dimensions of his or her upper body. The vertical adjustment is made by moving the stem up or down within the steering tube.

The rule of thumb for determining forward extension is to choose a stem that places the handlebars approximately the same distance in front of the saddle tip as the length of the rider's forearm, with fingertips outstretched. The tourer might want a bit less extension. The track racer would definitely want more—at least an inch more. The most common vertical position for the stem places the handlebars even with the top of the saddle. Touring cyclists might wish to have them a bit higher; track racers will almost invariably place them lower. Furthermore stems for track bikes are angled sharply downward, so the total effect is to place the bars very low indeed.

Stems for road and touring bikes are forged from aluminum alloys. Track stems, which bear a lot more stress, tend to be made from steel. The most popular alloy stems come from the factories of Cino Cinelli. Cinelli stems are light, strong, aerodynamic, nicely finished, and pretty to look at. Cinelli pioneered the sleek, bolt-less look in stems, countersinking the "binder" bolt and entirely

hiding the handlebar-securing bolt on his fanciest road stem by means of a very clever internal wedge system. On the less fancy stems, Cinelli and non-Cinelli, the handlebars are secured by a simple bolt, usually a countersunk Allen-headed one, that tightens the bracket that, in turn, grips the central portion of the bar.

The binder bolt that holds the stem in place within the steering runs from the bend down to the bottom of the stem, where it attaches to either a wedge-shaped nut that bears against the wedge-cut contour of the bottom of the stem, or to a conical nut that spreads the two flanges of the bottom of the stem, which in this case is split. In either case tightening the bolt causes the assembly to ex-

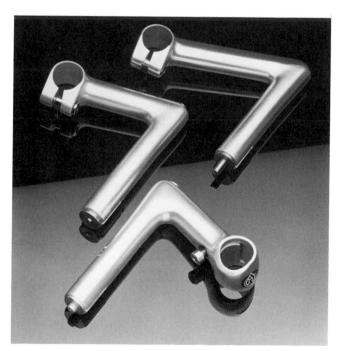

Handlebar stems of different extension lengths. The bottom stem, the Cinelli R/1, uses an internal sliding wedge mechanism to secure the handlebar.

pand one way or the other, thus fastening it securely inside of the steering tube. Following the lead of Cinelli, most manufacturers of stems now make the binder bolt a recessed hex-head type, so nothing projects to spoil the contour of the part or present a safety hazard.

There are basically three types of handlebars, corresponding to the three specialized types of bicycles: road racing, track racing, and touring. There are also a number of "general" drop-style handlebars that come as standard equipment on many non-specialized ten-speed bikes and therefore offer none of the special advantages of the more carefully adapted designs.

Track bars, unlike bars for other bikes, tend to be made from light steel tubing. The

aluminum alloys used for road and touring bars just aren't strong enough to withstand the forces generated by track sprinters, who use their arm, shoulder, and back muscles as well as their legs in pedaling. Also, since there is almost no occasion for the track racer to be in any but the lowest position, "on the drops," track-bar bends do not provide any other particularly comfortable or convenient hand positions. The bend starts virtually from the stem-attachment point. The drop is usually more pronounced than that on road handlebars, and the most comfortable position is generally on the ends of the "drops," a place where the road racer or tourist rarely places the hands. It is not the most desirable position from the point of view of rider comfort,

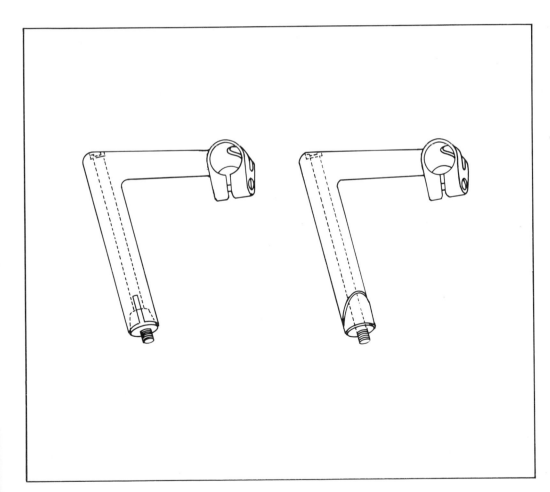

The two common binder bolt systems: wedge and cone.

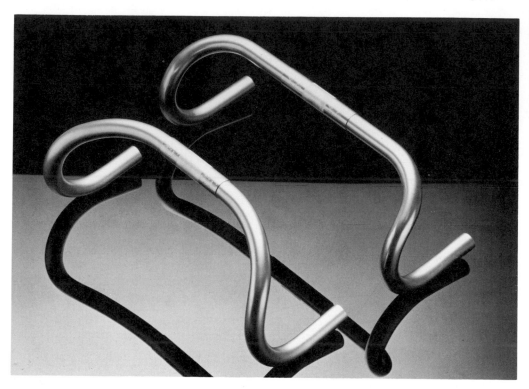

Typical road (top) and track handle-bars.

but then that's not what track racing is about. It does offer the greatest mechanical advantage, maximizing pedaling power.

Handlebars for road bikes are straight across for a good portion of their width; that is, horizontal and perpendicular to the main axis of the frame. The bars then make a sweeping bend forward, then downward, and backward. Four or five normal hand positions are made comfortable: first, on the horizontal part of the bars; next, and more common, on the frontward bend; third, on the downward bend, usually with a portion of the hands resting on the brake housings; fourth, similar to the third, with the thumb section resting on the brake hoods, the rest of the hand grasping the front of the housing or the levers; fifth, on the drops but high, within reach of the brake levers.

Touring handlebars, also frequently referred to by the French term *randonneur*, are more similar to road bars than to track bars. In fact they go, if anything, the other way.

The primary difference is the upsweeping bend starting at the center where they attach to the stem. This makes the hands-on-top position the most comfortable for the touring rider. It is a slightly less efficient position from the pedaling-efficiency point of view, but the comfort-for-efficiency trade-off is perfectly consistent with the aims of touring.

As mentioned, road and *randonneur* bars have been made from light aluminum alloys since the days in which these metals became available. The most sought-after, like the best stems, come from the workshops of Cino Cinelli. Handlebars were Cinelli's first marketed product after he retired from racing and went into the business of producing superior equipment for the racing cyclist. Cinelli's lightweight alloy handlebars represented the best available compromise between weight and strength when they first hit the marketplace in the late 1940s and, for most serious cyclists' money, they have stayed ahead of the field.

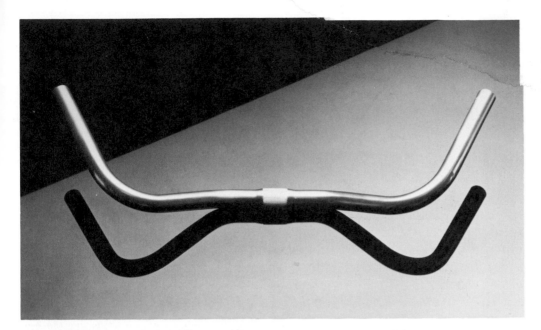

Some tourists prefer this type of handlebar which resembles a standard "street bike" utility bar.

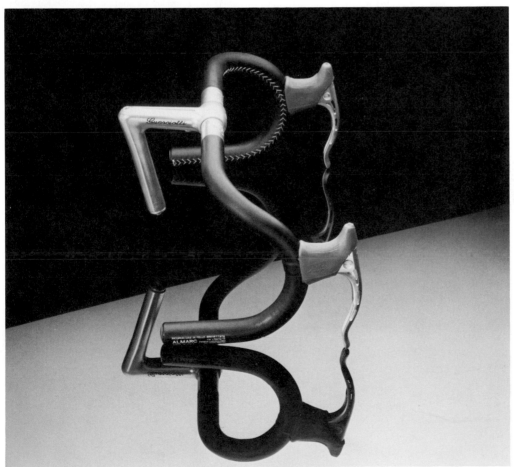

Guerciotti owners may purchase this handsome engraved handlebar set to complement their bikes.

SADDLES

From the point of view of rider comfort, the saddle is the single most important accessory of the bicycle—so it is surprising how long it has taken for the saddle to be understood clearly in terms of its form and function.

Until relatively recently fine bicycles all came with pretty much the same saddle, constructed of thick leather, suspended from a light steel frame. Most of these saddles were of rather narrow proportions, especially in the forward section. On more ordinary bicycles, saddles tended to be wider and more heavily padded. Why? Because that seemed logical to the people who designed them or perhaps to the people who bought them—they looked more like comfortable chairs. But things are not always what they seem. A bicycle saddle is not an easy chair.

Some careful analysis recently undertaken has made clear what the designers of those easy-chair saddles didn't seem to realize: Cyclists sit on their pelvic bones. Supporting the *gluteus maximus* has little to do with it. The forward-leaning position that is characteristic of all bicycles with drop handlebars of any style takes the buttocks more or less off the seat. What the leather saddles offered (after a few hundred miles of break-in riding) was a surface that molded itself to the contour of the pelvic bones and had some resilience or "give" to it, thus softening some of the jolts and bumps that are endemic to bike riding. The remaining virtue was in what was *not* there. In other words the portion of the saddle forward of the point at which the pelvic structure rests is only for balance, and the narrower the better. A wide structure there just gets in the way of the legs doing their thing.

The classic leather racing saddle.

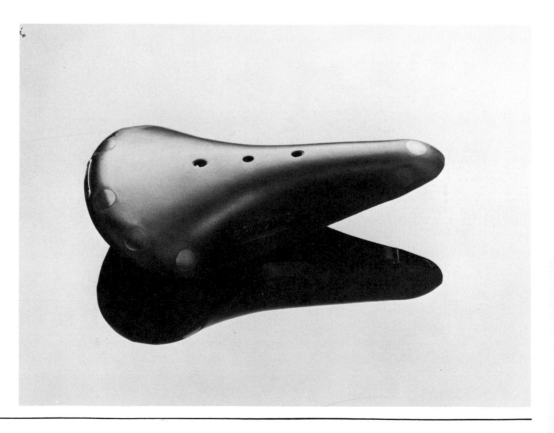

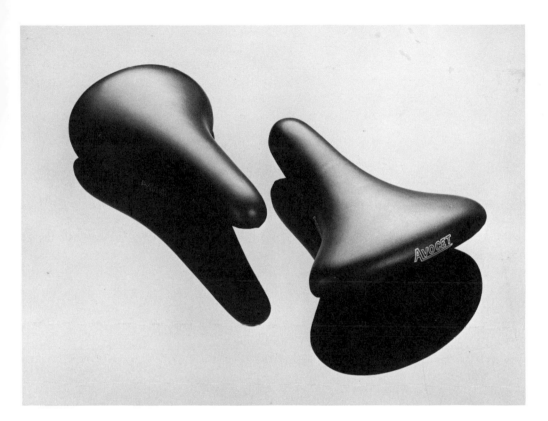

Avocet's new anatomic saddles: (left) men's racing, (right) women's touring.

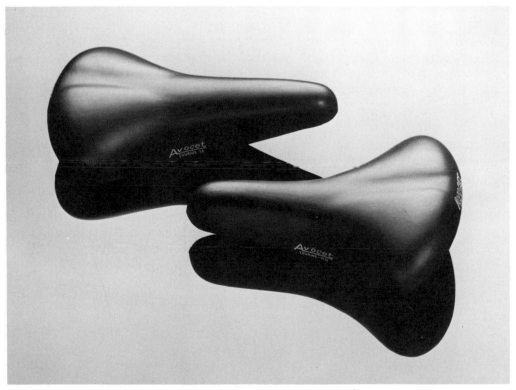

The second generation: the Touring II—men's (left) and women's.

Women's pelvises (right) are wider than men's; the new saddles take note of this fact, putting the "give" and the padding where the bones are.

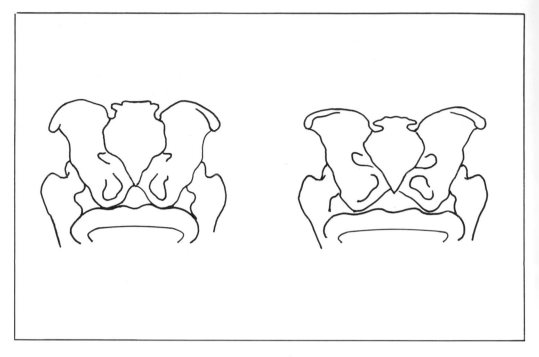

Good leather saddles are still available. They have the same virtues and the same drawbacks (mainly the breaking-in stage) that they have always had. But there is now a new breed. Thoughtful designers have devised new saddles using less costly synthetic materials and more efficient manufacturing techniques. The basic approach is to mold a flexible plastic or nylon shell that has thinner and therefore more flexible areas in the places where the pelvic bones make contact with the saddle. The degree of "give" is determined by the thickness of the material.

Despite the simplicity of manufacturing these new molded saddles, the prices of the better ones rival those of the best leather saddles. Why is this, you ask? Well, it's a sort of firmly established principle in our economic system that every time someone figures out a new, cheaper way to do something, it ends up being more expensive. In specifics, the nylon or plastic shell is only a shell—slippery and unabsorbent. Some sort of covering must be attached. The makers of the better molded saddles generally add a layer (or two) of foam padding and offer a selection of different covering materials, such as smooth leather, thick buffalo hide, suede or suede-like synthetics, shearling sheepskin, and the like. All of this is expensive but, most agree, better in the end.

One of the offshoots of the development of the new style saddle has been the recognition by one manufacturer at least (Avocet) that despite the raging controversey in the political arena, men and women are not created alike—physically. Most of the parts of the bicycle have been designed solely with the male body in mind, saddles included. But the average female's pelvic bones (we are always dealing in averages) are substantially more widely spaced than the average man's. This fact is now taken into consideration and has resulted in the production of a full line of saddles explicitly designed for women.

Aside from the anatomical advantages the new molded saddles offer another major benefit: weight saving. The lightest racing saddles in the new style are substantially less than *half* the weight of the old style leather saddles—even the superlight models that substituted titanium rails and frame for the normal steel, at three times the cost.

Saddles do not float in the air, regardless of their weight. A good seat post, a seemingly simple item, is actually a fairly costly component, costing as much as a good saddle or more. The best seat posts are cold-forged from aluminum alloys, combining lightness with strength as much as possible, like most components. Besides its obvious function of attaching the saddle to the bike, the seat post offers three modes of adjusting its position: vertically, by raising or lowering it within the seat tube; front-to-back, by loosening the clamp that holds the rails on the underside of the saddle and moving the saddle as needed; and in angle of tilt. The third of these adjustments is the trickiest. In inexpensive seat posts, a simple swivel joint is the most common solution. The faces of the meeting parts are knurled or serrated to prevent the parts from changing position once the assembly has been tightened. The knurling allows the seat to be positioned only at specific angles, determined by the width and angles of the serrations. While this may be acceptable for the average cyclist, increased precision and infinite adjustability was considered a necessity by a sufficient number of riders that the so-called micro-adjusting seat post is now the norm on fine bicycles. Although there are single-bolt adjustment systems, the more usual one uses two bolts, acting in opposition to each other to achieve and hold the desired saddle angle.

As mentioned, the vertical adjustment of the saddle is actually a function of the frame, not the seat post (except that the seat post must be long enough to allow sufficient upward extension and still leave enough inside the seat tube to keep the structural integrity of the whole). The seat lug and the tube underneath it are "split," and a clamp is fashioned, allowing the lug and tube to be tightened around the seat post by means of a bolt (which, nowadays, is usually a recessed hex-head bolt). One recent development, used primarily in team racing situations, is a quick-release lever (like that used on the wheel, but shorter, of course). This takes the place of the seat-clamp bolt and thus enables a rider to do an instant seat-height adjustment *while riding*, if necessary, in case he or she has to take over the bike of a teammate in an emergency.

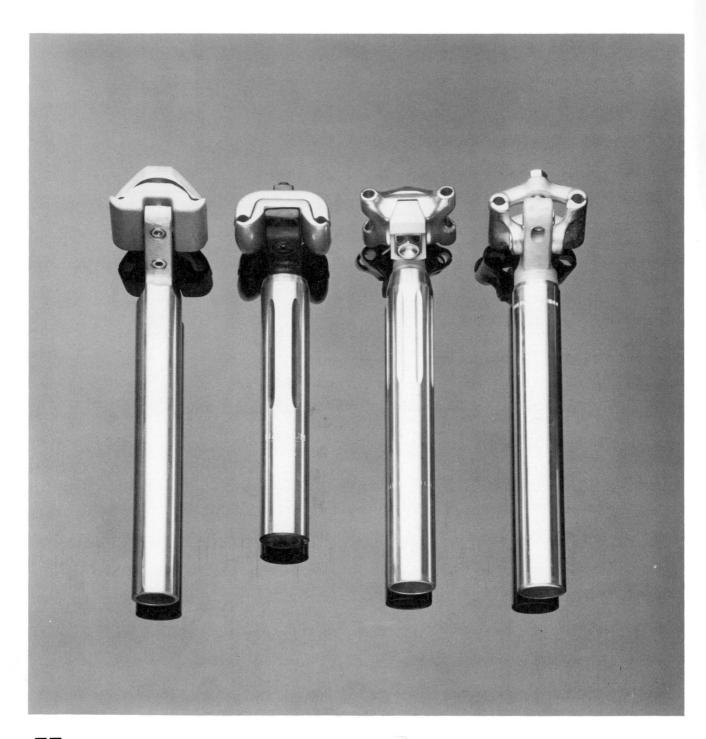

High-tech seat posts: (left to right) Avocet, 3 ttt, Campy Super Record, Campy Record.

THE DRIVETRAIN

Once the configuration of the safety bicycle became standardized, with the pedals connected to the driving wheel indirectly by means of a chain, designers and builders began to be able to concentrate more on improving and rethinking the component parts.

THE CRANK SPINDLE

The central point of power transmission in this now-standardized bicycle, the guts of the whole system, was the crank axle or spindle.

It has changed less, perhaps, than any other part of the bicycle—a massive bar of high-grade steel with bearing races milled into its basic profile. It is, as it was then, held in place within the transverse tubular housing known as the crank hanger or the bottom-bracket shell by bearing cups that thread into the outer edges of the bracket shell, and thus are adjustable to give the precise amount of clearance needed by the ball bearings. Retaining rings hold the cups in place once adjustment has been carried out. It is very much

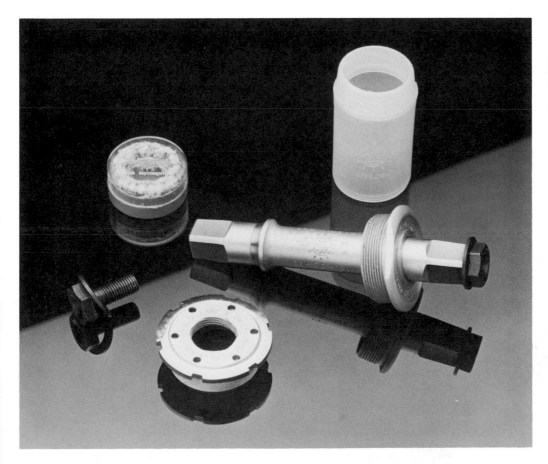

A conventional crank spindle set—the Campagnolo Record—with spindle (incorporating cones), balls, cups, lock ring, and protective plastic sleeve.

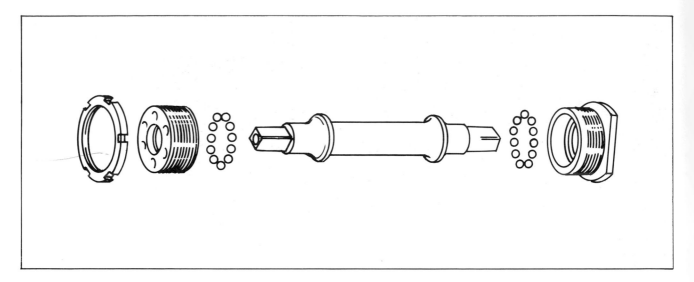

This schematic drawing shows how the parts fit together. The cups thread into the outer edges of the bottom bracket shell; the movable cup (left) is adjusted and held in position with the lock ring.

Cross section of a precision, sealed crank spindle bearing.

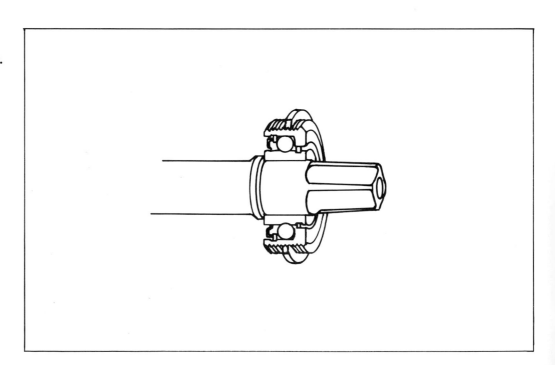

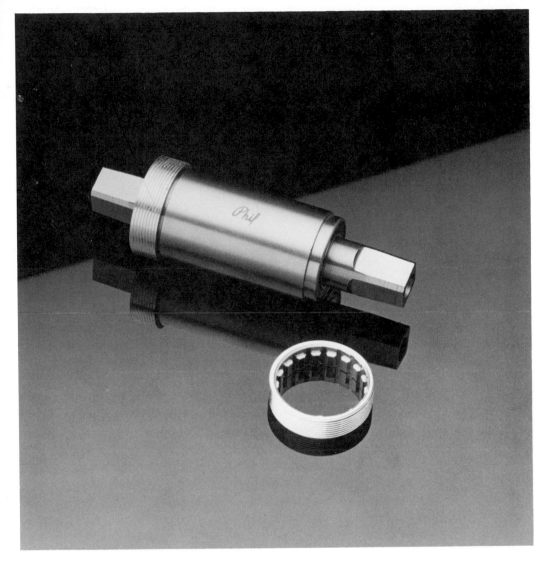

like a wheel-hub bearing assembly, but the parts are scaled to the job of dealing with hundreds of pounds of thrust. The maintenance required on the crank-axle bearings is simple enough. The bearings must be periodically dismantled, cleaned, regreased, reassembled, and adjusted, as with all such bearing assemblies, so that there is neither play nor binding in the assembly. How often this procedure is carried out depends on whether the bracket shell is perforated (as many are), on whether (if it *is* perforated) a plastic inner protective shell has been installed, and, generally, how much and how hard you ride.

One of the few changes in the crank-spindle assembly has been the introduction of the sealed precision bearing assembly as a substitute for the hand-adjusted system. The first such unit was designed by the U.S. designer, Phil Wood, who also pioneered the sealed-bearing wheel hub. Wood's bottom-bracket sets have become quite popular and, along with sealed-bearing axle sets offered

This super light Stronglight bottom bracket set features sealed bearings, titanium spindle, and light aluminum alloy cups.

more recently by other makers, seem to be the wave of the future. It seems to be the case that improvements, even if they are primarily improvements of convenience (as compared to performance), will be adopted regardless of cost. Sealed-bearing bottom-bracket sets tend to run about twice the cost of the equivalent set with conventional bearings. There is no appreciable difference in performance between sealed bearings and conventional cup and cone bearings.

One other innovation in the crank spindle came with the general move to titanium *everything,* when the space program and other large-scale technological drives brought the cost of the rare metal down to where it could be considered for such mundane applications as bicycle parts. Titanium spindles are made for a number of the better-known European bottom-bracket sets—at a cost of between three and five times the price of the steel unit it is replacing, with a weight saving of approximately 30 percent or an average of 100 grams (just over 3½ ounces).

CRANKS AND CHAIN WHEELS

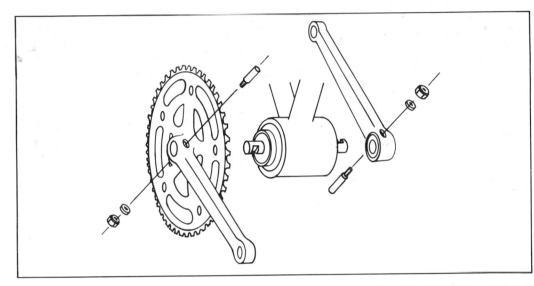

The old style: cottered cranks. Steel cotter pins hold steel crank arms to the steel crank spindle.

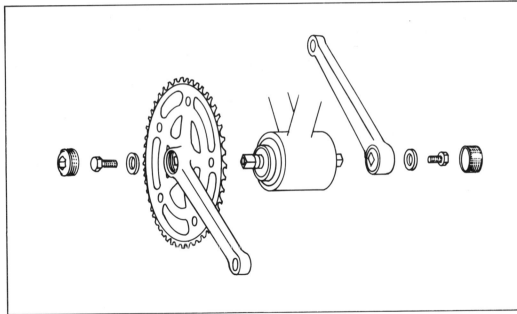

The new style. Steel bolts pass through the ends of aluminum alloy crank arms fixing them to the square-sectioned ends of the spindle.

Connected to the ends of the spindle are, of course, the cranks or crank arms. Up until about 1960 crank arms were made of steel. They fit over the ends of the spindle and were fastened in place by means of a steel "cotter," actually a tapered bolt, held in place with a nut. The end of the spindle, to which the crank arm fastened in this type of assembly, was cylindrical with a "flat" machined across one side to accommodate the cotter. The taper of the cotter bolt, when attached snugly, made for a very tight joint between spindle and crank.

With the extensive development and

Crank set by Gal-li of Italy.

use of aluminum alloys in bicycle-component manufacture, it was only a matter of time before they were used for cranks—and chain wheels. The weight saving was so significant that a way *would* be found. And so came about some significant alterations in the design of crank arms.

First, the new alloy cranks were a lot beefier—bigger in cross section to make up for the inherently inferior strength and stiffness. The method of attaching the crank to the spindle also had to be changed. Whereas steel was tough enough to stand the effects of a loose cotter   for a while at least—the aluminum would wear so rapidly under the same

circumstances that it simply wouldn't do. The solution that evolved with the first fine alloy crank sets is still in use. It is "cotterless" and, in addition to serving the purpose of attaching alloy cranks to a steel spindle without danger of unacceptable wear, it streamlined the look of the crank set—providing an aesthetic improvement while solving a practical problem.

All cotterless crank attachments follow the same basic design. The end of the spindle is formed into a slightly tapered square section and the end is drilled and tapped to receive an attachment bolt. The tapered square shank enters a square-sectioned mortice in

This crank set by Sugino of Japan is drilled for maximum weight reduction.

the inboard end of the crank arm and a bolt and washer, both steel, pull the arm onto the end of the axle. The bolt must be very tight indeed to prevent any play or the same sort of damage as from a loose cotter would result. The normal method of dealing with the potential problem is to retighten the bolts several times at short intervals until the bolts do not loosen up any more. Once tight, they generally stay tight. (The attachment bolt in a typical cotterless crank set is protected from dirt and moisture by a dust cap that screws on over the outside, installed and removed either with a hex key or a large screwdriver.)

Crank arms are not created equal, re-

gardless of their method of attachment to the spindle. The right-hand crank must transfer the torque from *both* cranks to the rear wheel, by means of the chain and *chain wheel(s)*. The chain wheel (on a track bike) or multiple chain wheel assembly (for road racing or touring bikes) connects with the crank system by means of a support commonly known as the "spider." The spider on a well-made crank set is almost invariably forged integrally with the right-hand crank arm—that is, they are formed out of a single piece of metal. (There is one exception to this.) This eliminates the possibility of any loosening or play developing between these two crucial

The Campagnolo Nuovo Record crank set—the racer's standard—and a Japanese contender for equal status—the Dura-Ace EX from Shimano. Notice the short or "W-cut" teeth opposite the crank arm, designed to facilitate releasing the chain in shifts from large to small chain wheel.

The TA Cyclo-touriste crank set—one of the few with a style definitely all its own. Probably the most important benefit of this arrangement is the extremely wide range of possible gearings.

drive components.

In the days of steel cranks the chain wheels and spiders were also made of steel. The typical arrangement on a high-quality crank set was a three-arm arrangement of the spider—three supporting and connecting arms led from the crank arm to the chain wheel. With the switch to lighter but less strong aluminum alloys, the number of legs on the spider increased from three to five. The vast majority of high-quality alloy crank sets have

five-armed spiders, this representing the best compromise between the requirements of strength and the goals of weight reduction. (There is, again, a single notable exception.)

On bikes with multiple chain wheels there must be some means of attaching at least one smaller, inner chain wheel to the assembly, sometimes two. Two systems have been in use for the past fifteen years. The first, followed by the vast majority of designs, attaches the outer and inner chain wheels to

The Cinelli VIP set—one of the early entrants into the luxury-appointments-for-bikes market— consists of the firm's finest handlebar and stem paired with a Unicanitor saddle. The ensemble is tied together by matching, color-coordinated suede leather coverings.

Frame maker's logos have spread from the frames themselves to various other parts of the bicycle in recent years. Ernesto Colnago was one of the first makers to put his symbol on the seatposts, chainrings, stems, etc., that came with built-up bikes from his shop.

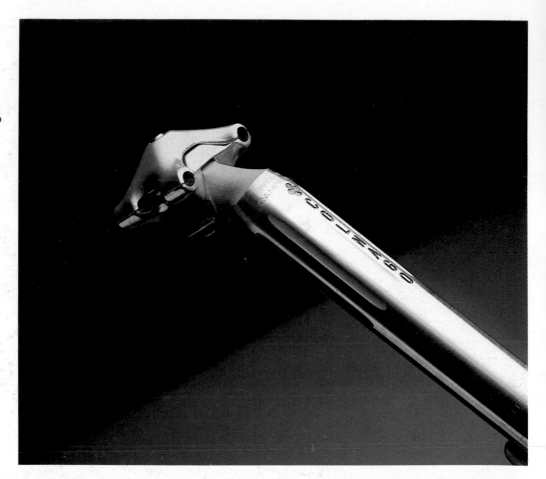

Anatomic saddles, new enough in themselves, are now aerodynamic and color-coordinated. This Concor 'Supercorsa' model comes in a selection of colors and different coverings. There is also a special, lightweight model available with magnesium mounting rails.

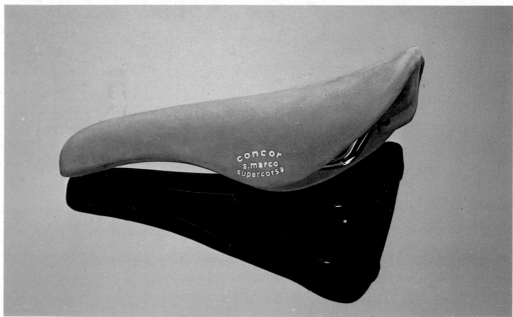

This engraved Guerciotti stem-handlebar set is another example of the same trend. It is a Cinelli stem and bar with the Campagnolo brake levers already mounted. The set is finished off with a cushioned, non-slip handlebar grip and the Guerciotti signature.

The Modolo Professional 'Stratos' brakeset is a side-pull design held by many to be superior in mechanical efficiency and quality of finish to its Campagnolo counterpart—not an easy reputation to earn in the cycling world. It is available in a range of colorful anodized finishes.

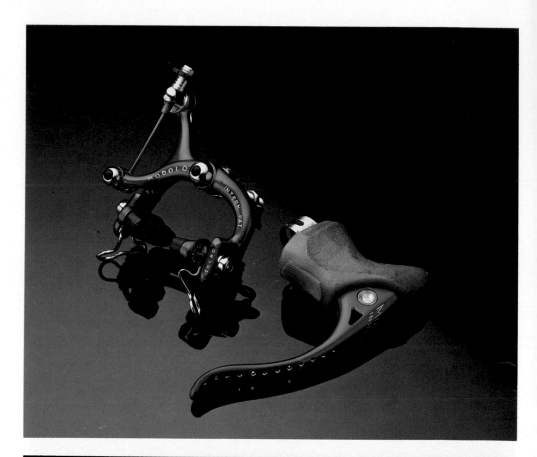

The Cinelli platform pedal reduces the pedal structure to the bare minimum, transferring the job of maintaining contact between foot and pedal to the shoe cleat. A projection on the cleat fits through the circular opening and is locked in place with the sliding lever.

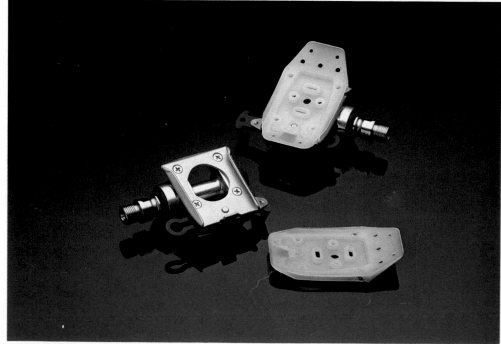

Innovative, high-tech brake levers/housings, also from Modolo. The design takes advantage of the possibilities inherent in molding high-impact plastics to make a lever that is strong, lightweight, aerodynamic, and better fitted to the human anatomy than most metal levers and housings.

Zeus, of Spain, has long been producing ultra-lightweight components, using aluminum alloys, titanium, and special construction techniques such as the drilling of the chainrings on this crankset for maximum weight reduction.

Galli is an Italian firm that has also aimed at the ultra-lightweight component market. This Galli crankset, a typical five-arm cotterless aluminum alloy unit, offers the attractions of a bright anodized finish and moderate price.

These aerody-
namic compo-
nents from Sun Tour
exemplify recent
trends in derailleur de-
sign, moving in the di-
rection of reducing
weight, bulk, and air
drag.

The long-await-
ed aluminum
alloy freewheel from
Campagnolo—a costly
but beautifully fin-
ished weightsaving op-
tion for the road racer.

the ends of the spider arms with a single set of bolts. This system is worked out in a number of different ways, depending on the range of chain wheel sizes that need to be accommodated. Sometimes the spider arms are long, which gives a lower limit to the size of the inner chain wheel somewhere around forty teeth. Other designs use short spider arms—which allow smaller inner chain wheels, but require the design of the outer chain wheels to be somewhat more elaborate for the sake of adequate strength. If provision has to be made for a third, yet smaller chain wheel, holes are drilled on the spider arms for the necessary attachment bolts.

All the exceptions to the design principles noted above belong to the design that uses the second system of chain-wheel attachment. All are features of the T.A. Cyclotouriste crank set. The Cyclotouriste system is the only one to use a non-integral spider; that is, it is integral with the outer chain wheel, *not* with the right-hand crank. The arm bolts to the outer chain wheel with five bolts. The outer ring of the main chain wheel is supported on a six-arm system. The two inner chain wheels (the set is designed primarily as a three-chain-wheel touring set) attach with a single set of six bolts near the base of the six support arms. What this system sacrifices in weight it makes up for in versatility. The completely interchangable inner chain wheels are available in every size from fifty down to twenty-six teeth, making possible a very wide range of gearings.

FRONT DERAILLEURS

Today's modern front derailleurs resemble their earliest forerunners quite closely. There has not been a great deal of change in the basic concept: Push the chain in the desired direction and the teeth of the adjacent chain wheel will pick up the chain, completing the shift—with the possible necessity of some final adjustment of the derailleur mechanism to make sure that the pushing part, the "cage," is no longer bearing against the chain once the shift has been made.

In the early days of derailleur use, when the standard gearing system was the "half-step" system, the differences in the circumferences (or tooth counts) of the two chain wheels were not very great. To engage the other chain wheel the chain had to make a journey of between ½- and ¾-inch vertically and ¼- to 5/16-inch laterally. A straight lateral push of the chain was adequate to accomplish the shift with reasonable efficiency. Thus the early front derailleurs operated on a very simple mechanism. The cage was mounted on a simple post that moved in or out as the movement of the shift lever determined. That was all.

With the switch to ever-greater ranges of chain-wheel sizes and the addition of a third inner chain wheel for touring, the chain had much greater distances to move and so front derailleurs were developed that coped better with the long-range chain-moving task. First was the problem of generating more cage movement for the limited amount of cable travel available. Second was the problem of facilitating the major vertical movement that the chain had to make, especially in the shift to a bigger chain wheel. These improvements are still being made. Derailleurs with improved shifting actions make their appearance each year, most using some sort of cam action to raise or "lift" the chain upwards as it pushes it outward. Cage design has also been reexamined from the point of view of its role in guiding the chain. Various shapes have been tried, along with the addition of protrusions on the inside of the cage that engage the chain and help to lift it off the smaller chain wheel and transfer it to the bigger, outer one.

Other improvements in front derailleurs have been in the standard directions of minimizing weight and in streamlining and making attachment easier. Virtually all high-quality derailleurs are now made from light alloys (or in some cases titanium, in part) except for the cage, which is still made of steel. So size and weight have steadily diminished over the years. Improvements in the mechanisms seem to be ever more subtle and the increments of improvement in performance are likely to be smaller and smaller. Further attempts to improve conventional front chainwheel shifting are beginning to look in other directions. We'll get to these in a bit.

REAR DERAILLEURS

Rear (as well as front) derailleurs are designed to handle specific ranges of gear changing capacity. The short-cage Campagnolo Record derailleur is designed for the narrow range of sprocket sizes used in racing. The Rally derailleur is designed for the wider range of sizes used in touring; its longer cage can "wrap" more chain.

In the ten- (or more) speed bicycle, the rear derailleur has a more demanding job to do than the front. It must have the capacity to make a number of changes, not just one (or two). This in turn requires that it move over a much larger distance. The operational principle is the same: Deflect the chain in one direction and the adjacent cog will eventually pick up the chain in its teeth and the chain will derail from the first cog to the new one. But the mechanism required to get all this done efficiently over the full range of five to seven sprockets is a lot more complex.

In modern rear-derailleur design the mechanism that actually guides the chain is a lot more efficient than the cage of the front derailleur, which simply shoves against the side of the chain to deflect in the desired direction (also lifting it, in certain designs). The rear derailleur actually *holds* the chain on a double-pulley system that acts as a miniature chain track. When the rear derailleur is operated, the chain is guided by two movable cogs in relation to five or more immovable ones, engaging or disengaging the latter at will.

But the rear derailleur has another function, less obvious than that of effecting sprocket changes, but just as vital. As the chain moves from one sprocket to another, or from one chain wheel to another, the effective *length* of the chain changes. The double-pulley system is responsible for reconciling these differences—for taking up slack or making more chain available as needed during gear changes. The two pulleys (known as the jockey, or guide, pulley and the tension pulley) are connected by a structure called the cage, which is pivoted so that it rotates in the same plane as the wheel (more or less). A spring tightens the tension pulley toward the rear (clockwise). The assembly thus acts as a chain reservoir, with slack being taken up by the spring action and released as shifting demands more chain. The amount of chain differential that the system can absorb, or "wrap" in bike

jargon, depends on the length of the pulley cage—the distance between the jockey pulley and the tension pulley. This is a deliberate design feature.

Rear derailleurs, then, are designed with rather specific ranges of gearing in mind. Their capacity to wrap chain is expressed in the total number of teeth between the largest and smallest numbers they can handle. The range runs from about a 22-tooth difference (12-tooth difference on the chain wheels plus a 10-tooth difference between the smallest and largest rear cogs) to a maximum of 36-teeth difference (16-tooth difference in front plus a 20-tooth difference in back). Along with this measure of the derailleur's capacity is a designation of the largest rear sprocket that the unit will accommodate. With these two numbers at hand it is possible to tell instantly whether a particular derailleur is suited to a particular gearing arrangement. In other words, not all derailleurs are created equal. In order to do their job better each is designed for a particular section of the gearing spectrum.

Most of the refinement in rear-derailleur design, aside from the specialization of gearing range (and the usual objectives of weight reduction and streamlining), have been in the direction of making the mechanism more rugged (simpler, less tempermental, and tougher) and on making shifting more positive and precise—less subject to "overshift" followed by a subsequent centering adjustment.

Now there are two distinct generations of derailleur design. The first, which includes most of the European designs, derive primarily from the early Campagnolo Gran Sport derailleur. At least they operate in much the same manner. The derailleur body moves in and out, laterally, from its pivot near the attachment point, maintaining a more or less parallel relationship to the wheel axle, by means of a parallelogram structure.

The newer generation, which includes

most of the Japanese designs, adds another movement or articulation: a diagonal action that keeps the distance between the jockey pulley and the freewheel cog more or less constant. Most testers and analysts agree that this makes for smoother, more precise shifting; most bike racers go on using Campagnolo derailleurs regardless.

Aside from the "slant-parallelogram" principle (which goes by other names as well), refinements in shifting characteristics have resulted from a number of factors including, precise tensioning, and, sometimes, ratcheting of the shifting levers, more careful design of the shifting cables and their paths (reducing the number of bends, the number of outer cables they must run through, and, generally, the amount of random friction they are subject to), and more careful tensioning of the internal mechanisms. A great deal of this refinement has been carried out by the Japanese firms Shimano and Sun Tour. Their derailleurs have gained wide acceptance among non-racing cyclists, but not, as yet, with racers, although both firms have gone after that market very aggressively. Time and better distribution of replacement parts may turn the tide toward the East.

One particular Shimano innovation that deserves mention here, although it is not available on any of their top-of-the-line derailleurs, is a device that allows shifts to be made with the levers while the bike is stationary. The shift is then actuated once the rider starts pedaling. Anyone who has had to start pedaling after an unexpected stop in a high gear (and that includes most of us) will appreciate the convenience of this idea. If public demand were sufficient, perhaps a similar feature might be incorporated into a sophisticated derailleur for touring or commuting.

CHAINS AND FREEWHEELS

The unheralded workhorse of the bicycle drivetrain is the chain. The chain revolutionized bicycle technology when it was first introduced as a drive mechanism in the mid-1880s, and its configuration was more or less perfected fairly soon thereafter. A properly lubricated chain with the typical modern roller-bushing-pin construction can transmit up to 98.5 percent of the power applied to it under ideal conditions (one of which is that the driving cog and the driven cog be in perfect alignment). That is a very impressive figure for *any* mechanical system.

While a bicycle chain is a very complex object in the aggregate, containing somewhere in the vicinity of 500 precision-shaped parts, most cyclists aren't impressed and don't give much thought to it except for lubricating it occasionally and replacing it every few years with a bright, shiny new one. Cycle component manufacturers, however, have been devoting some thought to chains—not so much in terms of technical specifications, since the strength and elongation of chains have long been quite satisfactory, but in terms of how they shift.

Back in the days of undisputed European domination of the bicycle-component market, one manufacturer, the Italian firm Regina, made most of the chains *and* most of the freewheels used by serious cyclists. The two products evolved as parts of a system. This established a pattern for later entrants into the field, and, nowadays, the notion that chains and freewheels are designed to operate *together* as a single system is a familiar one. This is not to say that *all* chains are designed or manufactured by companies that also make freewheels and other components (Sedis, for example, a leading chain manufacturer, does not) but there is a certain compelling logic to the idea that a systems-engineering approach should lead to improvement in this area.

Aside from such innovations as the (inevitable) titanium chain (produced by Regina, at about half the cost of a reasonable commuting bicycle), changes in chain design have

Bike chain is a "simple" arrangement of inner and outer link plates spaced by rollers and fastened by pins or rivets. The shapes, dimensions, tolerances, and physical properties of the component parts are crucial to a chain's performance.

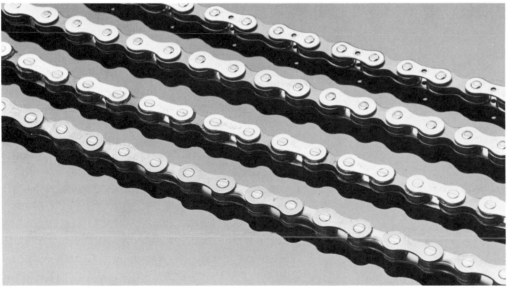

Four popular bicycle chains (top to bottom): Regina Corsa Oro, Regina Record Oro, H K K Ultra Six (for Sun Tour), Sedis.

related primarily to improving the interface between chain parts and the other parts they contact and adjusting the dimensions of the chain to the requirements of six- and seven-speed freewheels.

All chains designed to work with the new more-than-five-speed freewheels are, of necessity, narrower in their widest dimensions than older chains designed to work with five-speed clusters. But within this narrow world some chains have gotten even slimmer, some bigger. Sun Tour, for example, has reduced the thickness of the link plates on their new generation of chains (called "Ultra-6") and improved tooth clearance by beveling the inner surface of the outer links. (The latter feature also relates to shifting performance, as we shall see.) Shimano's "Uniglide" chain

Teeth on Shimano freewheels are beveled at the leading edge of the outboard side and at the trailing edge of the inboard side, producing a diagonal or "twisted" configuration that is aimed at improving shifting performance.

gets to something like the same place by taking an opposite route. The outer link plates on the Uniglide chain are bent outward, even with the heads of the link pins. This certainly improves tooth clearance between the plates *and*, Shimano reasons, gives the overall chain a much smoother bearing surface, reducing wear on a number of components (most certainly the front derailleur). This is the sort of development (along with micro adjustments in the basic dimensions of chain parts) that typifies efforts to improve chain design.

The other half of this duo of driving parts is the freewheel. One line of develop-

ment in the endeavor to produce more efficient, better shifting freewheels has been to experiment with the shape of the sprocket teeth. Better shifting systems have resulted.

The sprocket tooth has two different relationships to the chain—one when the chain is firmly seated, transmitting power; the other when the chain is being shifted. The part of the tooth that grips the chain in "normal" operation is the base. The design of this part of the structure was optimized long ago. The other part, the top of the tooth, has received a lot of attention recently.

In order for the chain to shift smoothly

and easily the configurations or "shapes" of the sprocket teeth and the insides of the link plates have to be such as to facilitate both release and engagement; the chain has to slide off easily and slip into the new position quickly and solidly. The Shimano Uniglide freewheel system employs an interesting innovation of this type. By cutting the teeth in what they call a "wave form," by chamfering the trailing surface of the tooth on one side (the outboard side) and the leading surface on the other side (the inboard side), they have done away with portions of the tooth that were in the way of efficient shifting—in one direction, from the smaller to the larger cog. In making a shift from a higher to a lower gear (from a smaller cog to a larger one) the axis of the chain is in line with the axis of the "twisted" tooth, and the release and reengagement of the chain take place with a minimum of fuss.

So what about shifting in the other direction? When shifting to the next higher gear (the next smaller cog), the chain stays firmly mated with the cog it is leaving a bit longer than with a conventional setup. The twist of the teeth is resisting the change. This eliminates a certain amount of slipping and bouncing that ordinarily accompanies upshifting. Then when the derailleur has moved far enough for the chain to be centered over the new cog, it drops into place quickly and solidly.

(Another Shimano innovation—the so-called alignment system wherein the spatial placement of teeth on adjacent cogs is supposedly optimized for most efficient shifting, allowing "the teeth to be closer to low side gears and high side gears in alternating sequence"–not only isn't an innovation, it isn't real, as far as I have been able to tell. The *spacing* of sprocket teeth is determined solely by the dimensions of the chain link. You can select a particular orientation of any two teeth on adjacent cogs, but the remaining teeth will come in and out of phase with this orientation in a totally mechanical and predictable manner that can't be influenced one way or the other by engineering, however clever.)

Sun Tour has done something similar in spirit to the Shimano twist tooth, but less radical. They have beveled the upper edges of the teeth to match the bevel on the inner surface of the link plates. This facilitates engagement and disengagement in a slightly more obvious way. Again, it operates only when the chain is being deflected and thus does not interfere with seating of the chain against the teeth in normal operation.

Other innovations in freewheel design relate to matters other than shifting performance. The switch from steel to alloy chain wheels created the expectation of a similar switch with freewheel parts, but it was a long time coming. The problem is that the wear on the freewheel is in direct proportion to the gear ratio being used at any given time. If the rear wheel is turning three times for each revolution of the cranks, then each tooth on the freewheel cog is engaging the chain three times as often as each chain wheel tooth. With a four-to-one gearing wear will be four times as great, and so on. Clearly the smaller the cog, the greater the wear ratio. The French firms of Maillard and Cyclo Pans were early entrants in the alloy-freewheel field. The latter (well-known for their simply engineered freewheel "kits" that allowed the cyclist to build freewheels with various combinations of interchangeable cogs) solved the wear problem by making the smallest cog, 13 teeth, in steel only. It was only in the 13-tooth cog that they found unacceptable wear. Regina has recently come out with an alloy freewheel in which the two smallest cogs are made out of, you guessed it, titanium (in addition to an all-titanium freewheel costing roughly ten times as much as their standard steel model). Campagnolo, after years of ex-

Literally years were spent developing and perfecting the manufacturing techniques that made the aluminum alloys, which are used in this lightweight freewheel cluster, sufficiently hard to meet Campagnolo's durability standards.

perimentation and development, has just put an alloy-freewheel set on the market. Once Campagnolo offers it for sale, you can be sure the bugs have been worked out.

The other big development is actually a reworking of the Cyclo Pan kit idea of easily interchangeable freewheel cogs giving the cyclist the opportunity to create his or her own gear ratios at will. Shimano, in the process of redesigning their rear hub and repositioning the freewheel side bearing, designed a new freewheel body that fit around the outside of the bearing. In addition to the convenience of changing cogs, the "cassette" freewheel offers some weight reduction and the possibility of using smaller cogs than have been possible (or used, anyway) on other freewheels: 11 and 12 teeth, allowing higher overall gear ratios or equal ratios with smaller chain wheels (but with greater wear).

Sun Tour has engineered a method of fitting a seven-cog cluster into the same space as a conventional six-cog, and a six-cog cluster into the same space as a five. This is accomplished by attaching the smallest, outboard cog in such a way that it projects outboard of the freewheel body, into what was formerly wasted space. It is significant in that the less space the freewheel takes up on the hub, the less the rear wheel will have to be dished. This seems to me to open up a line of development that I am not aware of anyone carrying out. It goes something like this. Six- and seven-speed clusters were introduced, leading to the development of a narrower chain so the cogs could be more closely spaced. Ways have been found to position the freewheel cogs more efficiently in terms of the wheel axle. Why not take these developments and, for those of us willing to figure out the gearings we need and made do with a

Shimano's 'Cassette' freewheel allows the cyclist to select the sprockets for his or her particular purposes and assemble the cluster that fits the bill. The smallest sprocket threads onto the body to lock the other, splined, sprockets in place.

five-speed rear, design a rear wheel that is even *less* structurally out of balance? It makes a lot of sense.

THE TEN-PITCH SYSTEM

So far this discussion of drivetrain components, their structure, design, and performance has related almost exclusively to multiple-gear bicycles—which, after all, constitute the vast majority of all bikes in the high-tech category. Track bikes, however, have a much simpler arrangement: lighter, simpler pedals; strong cranks; superstrong crank spindle; a single alloy chain wheel with the chain running to a single, fixed sprocket on the rear hub—no freewheel, no gears. Track chain wheels are available in the general range of 42 to 52 teeth. Rear sprockets most often used range from 13 to 16 teeth, offering the rider a choice of fixed gearings running from roughly 70 inches to 110 inches.

As track drivetrains are simpler than road drivetrains, they are also more efficient. They are lighter due to the lack of extra chain wheels—and the provisions for attaching and interchanging them—and, significantly, due to the reduced width of the spindle. The laying out of the chainlines on a track bike is much simpler. There is no need to make space to fit in multiple cogs, front or rear. Finally there is no energy loss from chain deflection. Chain wheel and rear sprocket are in perfect alignment at all times.

It's hard to imagine how this nitty-gritty, pared-down system could be significantly improved without going into totally new concepts. The Shimano Corporation has recently brought out a new line of track drive components, different from the other available track components in one specific, conceptual way: They are miniaturized.

What does that mean? First it is necessary to realize that the driving cogs on a bicycle are all calibrated in terms of the length of the chain link. The spacing of the chain links is the unit of measurement for these parts. That measurement has been standardized, since well before the turn of the century, at one-half inch—a very English standard. Shimano's 10 Series is based on a chain with links 10 millimeters long (compared to 12.7 millimeters—the metric equivalent of one-half inch). This means that the on-center spacing of the driving teeth on both front and rear cogs is reduced in the proportion 10:12.7. The size of the components is reduced, making them lighter, and—if the design is not otherwise altered—stronger, by virtue of being smaller. There is also a theoretical gain in mechanical advantage between the smaller chain wheel and the length of the crank. The mechanical advantage is determined by the ratio of the diameter of the chain wheel in relation to the length of the lever (crank arm) that turns it. The longer the crank or the smaller the chain wheel, the greater the mechanical advantage.

The transmission capacity of the miniaturized components is, theoretically, unaltered. The gearing is certainly not changed. That is strictly and simply a matter of arithmetic. Performance, then, should be equal. The components are undeniably lighter, reducing overall mass; and they are, theoretically, stronger and more rigid, due to their reduced dimensions. It seems too simple and too good to be true. There must be a trade-off somewhere. And, of course, there is: Wear is increased significantly. Though miniaturized components had actually been tried before by European manufacturers, they abandoned them for that reason. Therefore, the idea now seems to be an innovation.

There are, however, real advantages to the use of these smaller components. Perhaps the advantages are not entirely free from compensating disadvantages, but they sound good and they look good on paper. For the world-class racer, especially one whose equipment is being paid for by someone else, Shimano's 10-millimeter pitch components should be a boon.

BRAKES

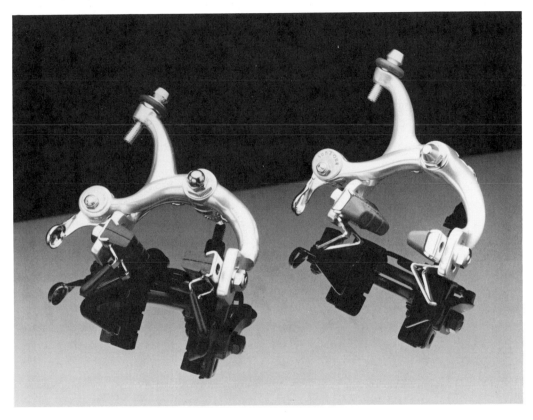

If imitation is the sincerest form of flattery, the Campagnolo brake should be extremely flattered. This Sun Tour model is only one of many attempts to duplicate the legendary Campy virtues.

Why have I chosen to discuss brakes all alone, off in a corner by themselves? Well, partly because they don't seem, somehow, to relate to any other system in the bicycle. They are, after all, the only part of the bicycle designed to make it go slow rather than fast. However, the faster you do go on a bicycle, especially in any kind of traffic, the more surely you need to be able to slow it down.

It was actually quite a while after the idea of the bicycle had taken hold that anyone thought of putting a brake on one and, to tell the truth, the brakes on most early bicycles were pretty much of an afterthought. By the 1880s most bicycles had brakes (in Britain especially they were required by law), but the design usually employed was the so-called spoon or roller that slowed the bike by bearing against the rear tire—not a very efficient arrangement. People were clearly still more

New molded brake levers and housings from Modolo of Italy are light, comfortable, and mechanically efficient.

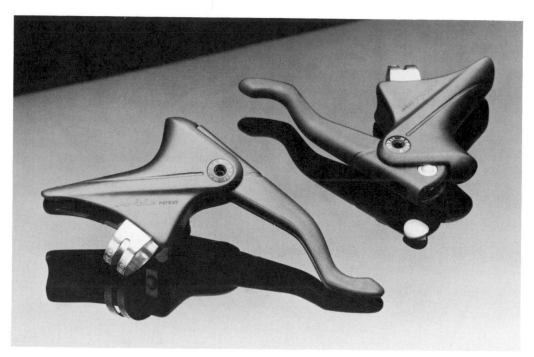

interested in going fast than going slow. It was really not until after the turn of the century that the internal, expanding-hub "coaster" brake and the "rim-caliper" brake were developed, becoming the normal solution to the stopping problem for the duration.

The coaster brake, still found on the standard "paper-route" bike is pretty efficient, but it and the hub necessary for it to work are too heavy for high-performance bicycles. There *are* other types of brakes in use on fine modern bikes, but these are mostly rather specialized—such as the "disc" brakes used on some tandem bicycles (which, after all, has to handle the weight of *two* riders), and so on. It is the caliper brake that is our subject here.

Caliper brakes have been made in two distinct styles for a good many years. In the "centerpull" brake the two arms or calipers are pivoted on opposite sides of a central bridge or mounting plate. The ends of the two arms are joined, usually with a section of wire brake cable, sometimes long, sometimes short. This "saddle" is in turn attached to the cable coming from the hand-brake lever.

Squeezing the lever causes an upward pull on the ends of the caliper arms and forces the other ends (and the shoes or pads) against the rim.

In the "sidepull" brake the two arms are pivoted in the center of the configuration. A housed cable runs to the upper caliper arm, where the housing ends, and the cable runs through and down to the lower arm. When the lever is squeezed it shortens the length of cable separating the two arms, forcing them together, and forcing the other ends of the arms against the wheel rim. (Actually most of the movement is of the lower arm in relation to the upper, but the upper does move a bit.)

The two types of brakes are similar in that increasing the "reach" (or the length of the calipers in general) increases the amount of "slop" resulting from the flexibility of the material. (All good brakes are made from light aluminum alloys these days.) When the sidepull brake is made with a "short reach"—that is, when the design of the mounting in relation to the rim allows the caliper arms to be short—it gives a very precise, positive-feeling

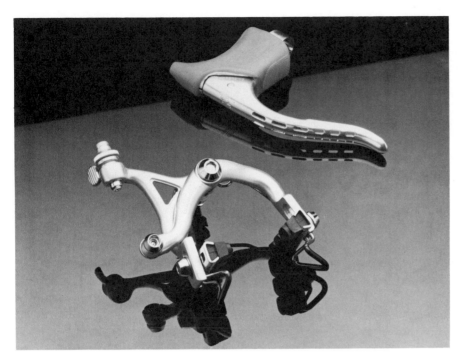

This well-fin-
ished, light-
weight, forged Dura-
Ace brake is Shi-
mano's top-of-the-line
"conventional" side-
pull.

braking action. The centerpull design, however, has a couple of inherent advantages (advantages seldom fully realized in production
models). First is an inherently more balanced
application of braking pressure from the two
arms. The force is distributed evenly from the
brake lever to the two calipers and braking is
smooth even if the wheel is not true. More
significant, perhaps, is the theoretically better
position of the pivot or fulcrum points in the
centerpull brake. The pivots are much closer
to the working ends of the calipers, giving a
decidedly greater mechanical advantage. In
many, many designs, however, this potential
advantage is partly or totally compromised by
the fact that the long lengths of stretchy wire
cable used to activate the mechanism make
the overall action "spongy."

Both types, then, are mechanically
sound, with certain advantages and disadvantages. However, the sidepull brake has dominated the field of fine bike components—totally. Why? The answer is not entirely clear.
What is clear is that Campagnolo designed a
very precise, carefully engineered and manu-

factured sidepull that immediately thereafter
became the standard by which all others measured their products. The "Campy" brake is a
fine brake. It is reliable and efficient. Other
manufacturers have been copying it for several decades now.

Shimano, however, with their methodical approach to bicycle engineering, took another look at the centerpull alternative, taking note of the inherent advantages
mentioned above. They worked on solutions
to the *dis*advantages of centerpulls, first coming up with a way of tightening up a relatively inexpensive model. But their *pièce de
résistance* is the "Parapull" brake. In the
Parapull the upward motion imparted by the
brake cable has been turned directly into outward motion. The saddle of wire cable has
been eliminated, also eliminating much of the
"softness" in the conventional force-trans-
fering system. In the Parapull brake, the brake
cable is fastened to a triangular *cam* against
which the upper ends of the calipers rest. As
the lever is squeezed, the cam is pulled upward, spreading the ends of the arms outward,

rapidly and positively, with *no* lost motion. The shape of the cam accounts for the fact that more caliper movement results from a given movement of the brake lever than in conventional design of either side- or center-pull styles. (This allowed Shimano to eliminate the complicated quick-release mechanism necessary on most brakes to facilitate wheel removal. The calipers on the Parapull can rest far enough apart in normal usage so as not to interfere with wheel removal and still act responsively enough to stop the bike faster than anything else around.) As with most things, the old way worked well and the new way may not make *that* much practical difference; but, to me, it is exciting to see a brilliantly simple piece of design made into a reality.

SOME COMMENTS ON THE CAMPAGNOLO QUESTION

There are a great many cyclists who will tell you without batting an eye: "If Campagnolo makes it, buy it. It is the *best*!" S.P.A. Brevetti Internazionali Campagnolo (the full title of the entity fondly known as "Campy" on these shores) is one of a very few firms manufacturing bicycle components whose market is *not* primarily what is called in the trade "original-equipment manufacturers"—components for production bikes. There are production bicycles that use Campy equipment—practically every manufacturer's top-of-the-line model does—but Campagnolo's main market is individual cyclists and teams, the world over.

The excellence of the products produced by Campagnolo is so legendary that it does not seem to occur to many people that any other equipment might be satisfactory. While this attitude certainly originated with racers, it is often echoed by cyclists who have never ventured near a bicycle race, let alone competed.

In any case, to understand why Campy equipment is so highly regarded, you need to know something about what is behind it. Signor Campagnolo has, from the very start of his design career, been an absolute perfectionist. He started out as a racer and understood a racer's need for equipment that measured up to the highest possible standards. He would typically spend years, if necessary, perfecting a design before ever offering the component for sale. That is an unusual attitude in the business world.

Then, once the designs are approved and sent out into the world to do their work, they are subject to constant reevaluation, and small, often invisible, changes and improvements are made. Campagnolo has the input of practically the entire European racing community, and he *uses* it. Further, Campagnolo's manufacturing and quality control standards are—well, beyond reproach. Put this all together with very extensive distribution and availability of replacement parts and you have a combination that's hard to beat.

So wherein do we presume to argue with the "If-Campy-makes-it, buy-it" dictum? Well, there are several considerations you might wish to mull over. First of all, Campagnolo equipment is the most expensive—often by a factor of two or more. That may influence some potential customers. The quality is worth paying for, of course—if you need it, either for practical or for psychic reasons. The most vociferous advocates of Campagnolo equipment are, as I said, bicycle racers. Despite the fact that this advocacy often takes on the character of a religion, I am willing to accept that for them it is true. Racers regularly punish their equipment in ways that recreational riders rarely do: they demand a lot, and Campy's reputation for virtual indestructibility is well-earned. But my purposes (and yours) are not necessarily the same.

Second, Campagnolo's approach *is* basically conservative. The fundamental designs remain decade after decade (the ever-popular Nuovo Record Derailleur was designed 20 years ago or more). The engineers at Campagnolo are willing to take infinite pains to make each component as good as it can be—not a bad philosophy—but they do not seem to be looking for any *new* answers. Meanwhile many other dedicated engineers and designers have been striving to come up with designs that—dare I say it—work better. It would be foolish to suppose that all those efforts had failed to produce any improvements.

It may be an emotional prejudice on my part in favor of a pluralistic world, but I hope (and expect) that other component manufacturers will move in the direction of responding to critics and removing some valid complaints and in so doing become more truly competitive.

Having examined the bicycle in such minute detail, we may well be in danger of not being able to see the forest for the trees. All of that anatomical detail is interesting (you say), but what does it all add up to? A bicycle, maybe? Well, yes, as a matter of fact. But there are as many ways to build and equip a bicycle as there are ways to avoid paying your income taxes.

BIKES FOR ALL REASONS

The following are some loosely related thoughts on real bicycles and their components (as opposed to two-wheeled, dissecting-room specimens), and some of the considerations that might go into selecting one set of possibilities over another.

Most of the dedicated bicycle fanatics I know and see around—especially the ones who race, or work out, at least—own machines that proudly display the names and logos of famous European (nowadays mostly Italian) frame builders; the equiva-

lent, surely, of wearing fine tweeds tailored by one of the prestigious firms on London's famous sartorial strip, Savile Row. But what do you get when you buy a tailor-made bicycle (or suit) besides prestige?

Well, for one thing (as

any of those fanatics would tell you), it is a guarantee that you are buying the finest materials and workmanship—or at least it *should* be. The quality of the materials, of course, is just a starting point—a point from which anyone can start. The workmanship is what *really* counts. We looked briefly at some of the reasons for the absolute necessity of careful workmanship in high-grade alloy steel bicycle frames in the anatomy section.

For the strength of the material (the steel) to be preserved and maximized in the finished frame, the tubes must be cut and mitered very accurately and heat must be applied judiciously in the brazing process. The more heat used in brazing, the greater the strength loss in the steel and the greater the likelihood of the formation of crystalline structures in the grain of the metal. These

structures have the potential of becoming fracture planes in a crash or other sudden stress. The cooling of the brazed assemblies must also be carefully controlled or the frame is likely to be warped and out of line. So then any sloppiness or slip-up in the fitting and assembly of the bicycle frame is likely to detract from the integrity of the finished product. Most serious cyclists are convinced, and not without reason, that the kind of skill, knowledge, and conscientiousness needed to turn out a really fine frame are in fairly short supply. Pride has a lot to do with it. (There are other points of pride in workmanship having to do with the quality of the finish, but that's really secondary. There are many workmen capable of putting a beautiful coat of paint over a poorly made frame.) So much for Answer One.

Answer Two (from the

same fanatic) is that you are buying, in addition to a well-made product, a design philosophy. Each builder has particular notions about how a bicycle works best and why. In the case of several European builders—especially, again, the Italians—these notions are derived from first-hand racing experience. The philosophy is expressed in what has come to be called the geometry of the frame—its configuration, proportioning, tube angles, fork design.

Almost anyone but a professional racer is likely to choose a design philosophy by reputation, rather than by hands-on comparison. It is expensive and time-consuming to try out one special-order frame after another. At some point you just have to ride. In any case, design philosophy is intangible, but it *is* something—like style—that matters. So much for Answer Two.

FITTING THE FRAME TO THE RIDER

Your fanatic advisor might well go on to give you Answer Three. When you buy a made-to-order bicycle, you get a tailor-made fit. Now virtually every writer on the sub-

ject (as well as coaches, salesmen, and kibitzers in the park) agree that a proper fit is important if one is to be happily mated with one's bicycle. But what *is* a proper fit, you

may ask? As a matter of fact, you may *well* ask. There is a considerable diversity of opinion on this question. Here is a sampling of systems, drawn from readily available sources, that describe the proper relationship between the size of various body frame parts and various bicycle frame parts.

System 1. Pick your proper frame size by first straddling the seat tube to make sure you have comfortable clearance, then measuring your inseam (standing on the floor in stocking feet), and selecting a frame with a seat tube measuring 9 or 10 inches less than the inseam measurement.

System 2. Measure leg length (in stocking feet) from the floor to the "head" of the femur. (The femur is your thigh bone and its head is essentially your hip joint.) Proper frame size is a seat tube 13¾ inches less than your leg measurement.

System 3. Measure from floor to head of femur and subtract 12¾ inches, *or* measure inseam and subtract 9 inches (to get seat-tube length).

System 4 (developed by the Italian Central Sports School, abbreviated CONI). Determine seat-tube length by measuring your lower body length from the floor to the pubic bone (in stocking feet, as always). The proper seat-tube length is then picked from a table (apparently empirically derived). The actual seat-tube lengths run from 63.75 percent of the body measurement for the

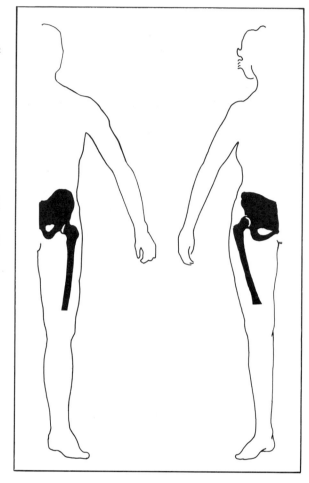

Meticulous fitting of frames to forms requires that a number of body measurements be taken into consideration. Many custom frame builders use anatomical charts like these to ensure a perfect frame fit. Statistically, women's legs are longer and their torsos are shorter than men's.

smallest frames to 62.1 percent for the largest. The top-tube length is determined by measuring the torso from the pubic bone up to the sternum (breastbone) *and* arm length from the tip of the shoulder blade to the wrist bone. The two measurements are added together and the top-tube length is, again, selected from a table. Actual top tube lengths run from 53 percent of the combined body measurements for the smallest frames to 48 percent for the largest.

To be fair it must be pointed out that the first three systems assumed that the reader would be buying a stock frame, hence no consideration of top-tube length. The last system is more along the lines of how a custom-frame builder would go about proportioning a frame for you. In fact that may be one of the significant benefits of ordering a custom-built frame: Along with the rest of the design philosophy you are buying the builder's concept of how a frame *should* fit. Any custom builder worthy of the name will certainly base the design of your frame on a set of measurements he or she feels are crucial. For the most careful and precise fitting of frame to rider, such as that that takes place in outfitting professional racing teams, the builder must be familiar not only with the anatomical details but also with the individual's personal riding style, so that riding position and weight distribution can be adjusted to take maximum advantage. But that's another story. Few of us will ever command that degree of attention from a frame builder.

That's one side of the coin; let's take a look at the other. I happen to know that a good number of those serious bike fanatics got their fine frames, not by writing off to Cinelli, Colnago, Pogliaghi, or Guerciotti, but off the walls and ceilings of a half-dozen local bike shops that keep them in stock. That would seem to do away with Answer Three. This is I suppose the distinction between the handmade bicycle and the made-to-order bicycle. What is the point of buying a handmade frame that is not precisely fitted to your body? How feasible is this notion? Well, it depends very much on how close to "average" proportions you happen to be. I was lucky for instance. I bought my frame long before

I knew anything about the intricacies of frame fitting. I am of fairly average build and it just so happens that both of the critical tube lengths are within less than a centimeter of being right on, according to the CONI tables.

If you happen to be unusually long legged (or short legged), if you are a woman (stock frames are based almost universally on average *male* proportions), if you are unusually large or small, a stock frame probably won't fit you very well. You would probably be better off going to the trouble and expense of obtaining a made-to-order frame.

For those of us who seem to fit stock frames pretty well, this opens up another can of worms. If a stock frame from a custom builder is acceptable, what about a stock frame from a non-custom builder? (As a matter of fact, the builder of perhaps the most expensive bicycles in the world [Gary Klein] offers a made to order frame only at such an extraordinarily high price [$6,560] that it is hard to imagine he ever gets an order for one. His bicycles are stock-frame sizes.)

There is a new trend in the bicycle business. The efficiencies of mass production are being combined with the precision of intensive quality control in a number of attempts to turn out stock

frames of very high quality at some savings in labor—basically an attempt to have the best of both worlds by means of compromise. The Medici Bicycle Company (U.S.A.) is an example of this approach—production frames, frame sets, and finished bicycles, all of the highest quality materials and, presumably, workmanship with some choice of components in the complete models. Assuming that price and availability compare favorably to the custom-built frame or stock frame from the custom builder, this seems to open up an additional option for the customer who wants custom quality at a non-custom price. Time and the idiosyncrasies of cyclophiles alone will determine if the market for this type of frame is a viable one.

Just to end this discussion on a slightly less serious note, I hasten to add that many, many experts—coaches, builders, *and* kibitzers—agree that for more than 98 percent of all riders it is the condition of the rider that is the most crucial *variable* in determining performance, not the intricacies of frame fit. There is a real split between the "just subtract 10 inches from your inseam" school and the "get it right, down to the nearest millimeter" school. Each—on the level that they are dealing—is right.

FITTING THE FRAME TO THE RIDE

The purposes of the general cycling enthusiast, the rider who maybe does a bit of club racing, a bit of day-touring, and basically just enjoys being on a fine bike, are almost certain to be served by any number of high-quality "production" bicycles, available at a fairly wide range of prices. However, there are those for whom the production bicycle is not the answer. The reason that some cyclists go to custom builders—and create enough business to enable builders to thrive as specialist handcraftsmen—is that they need something special, something otherwise unavailable.

Once you arrive at the point of creating a bicycle that is uniquely your own—made in your image, as it were—a bicycle that originates as an order on a custom-frame builder's desk, you will be required to answer a number of questions. Many of these will probably be about the size and shape of your body, more or less along the lines outlined previously. Some of the questions may be about your riding style, but the *fundamental* question will be, "For what purpose is

this bicycle required?" (I.e., what kind of riding are you going to do on it?) Custom-made bicycles, then, tend to be specialized machines, built for particular purposes. Traditionally frame styles have fallen into three distinct types: road racing, track racing, and touring.

Though there are some differences among the structures of the three types of frames (fork section, tube gauges, chain lines, etc.), the most important differences from the design point of view are in the configurations of the frame: the angles and dimensions of the tubes and stays; the rake of the fork. There is a rather limited spectrum of geometrical possibilities in building the conventional frame—a limited range of dimensions that will give anything like optimum performance. The track-racing bicycle and the touring bicycle tend to use dimensions and angles at opposite ends of the spectrum, with the road bike somewhere in between. Let's take a minute to summarize the salient features of the three types of specialized bicycles.

TRACK BIKE DESIGN

The *raison d'être* of the track-racing machine is rapid acceleration and maximum speed, achieved under relatively ideal conditions. These are achieved primarily by keeping weight, especially rolling weight, to a minimum while designing the frame for maximum torsional rigidity. (Actually anything in the whole system that flexes, wastes pedaling power—cranks, chain wheel, toe straps, handlebars) Frame rigidity (mostly resistance to bottom-bracket sway) results from shortening the wheelbase of the cycle, most particularly by shortening the chain stays. A bike with a short wheelbase tends to have steeply angled seat and head tubes. In addition to shifting the distribution of weight forward (as compared to other types of designs) this has some secondary effects. First, it diminishes the shock-absorbing capacity of the frame tubes, making for a bike that feels "nervous" or "frisky" but is often described as fatiguing to ride. Second, the steepness of the head tube, particularly, influences the steering characteristics of the bike. The steeper the head angle, the less trail inherent in the system. (Trail is the distance between where the steering axis intersects the ground and where the wheel actually touches. The more trail, within limits, the greater stability—the more the bike tends to continue going in the same direction.) Less trail means more responsive steering, but that also means more control, more effort on the part of the rider. Finally, the shortening of the overall shape of the bicycle, if carried too far, can create clearance problems between the pedals and toe clips and the front wheel. Since the riding conditions are pretty close to ideal (cycle tracks or velodromes are smooth and steeply banked; sudden sharp turns usually aren't necessary) a lot of the potential difficulties resulting from the extremities of design are avoided, the trade-offs are acceptable.

TOURING BIKE DESIGN

The most important characteristics of a touring bicycle are rider comfort and stable, predictable handling under loads—virtually the opposite

of the track bike. Sheer speed is *not* a primary objective. Lightness and speed are desirable, all things being equal, but less important than either safety or comfort. Frame strength is important, of course. Although the touring cyclist is not likely to test the strength of his or her frame *in quite the same way* as a track racer, it *will* be tested—as will the wheels— by the extra load and the roughness of the terrain traveled over.

Both comfort and stable handling are enhanced by selecting a longer wheelbase; which, in turn, means shallower tube angles. This means an increase in the shock-absorbing capacity of the diagonal frame tubes, a backward shift in weight distribution, and inherently more stable steering—a complete reversal of all these factors with respect to the track bike. The stretching out of the geometry also provides another element critical to the cycle tourist for safety's sake: clearance—clearance between tires and frame tubes for mudguards, clearance of the front wheel for pedals and toe clips, clearance to the rear between the rider's heels and the panniers.

The question of stability has to do with more than steering in a touring bike. Since the bicycle will be called upon to carry as much

as thirty or forty pounds of baggage in addition to the weight of the rider, the lower the overall center of gravity the better. So, along with the long wheelbase, touring bikes tend to be designed with low bottom brackets. The attachments for all of the luggage (and other accessories) must be secure and kept as low to the ground as practical. A full complement of touring carriers usually includes low carriers (panniers) in back and a handlebar pack (or sometimes front panniers) in front. Other light gear may be stowed over the rear wheel if necessary. All heavy objects should go as close to the ground as possible. All payload must be kept as immobile as possible. Moving objects—objects moving *relative* to the motion of the bike—generate their own momentum and are experienced as "dynamic" loads by the rider. (Anyone who has ridden a bike carrying heavy things in a book bag or similar container hanging from the handlebars has some idea of the havoc this swinging weight can cause.) In any case the bicycle must have secure attachment points for *all* gear, from panniers to pumps and water bottles and generator lighting. This is usually managed by means of brazed on bosses or mountings for each rack and piece of equipment.

Finally, touring bikes need wide-ratio gearing. (This

is not a feature of the basic frame design, but it *is* a necessity.) The tourist tends to frequent hilly places and is usually carrying a lot of extra weight. Link this with the fact that he or she is there to have fun rather than to compete, and the necessity of a gear range starting down in the mid-to-low thirties becomes clear.

ROAD RACING BIKE DESIGN

Midway between those of the track bike and the touring bike lie the purposes and the designs of road-racing bikes.

The road racer would dearly love to combine the attributes of track and touring bikes into one machine: lateral rigidity, good acceleration, a comfortable ride, and stable, reliable handling. Unfortunately so far no one has been able to put all those elements into one package. In the world of bicycle building art lies in finding the best possible compromise for a given situation. The operative concept, once again, is trade-off: a little less of this for a bit more of that and vice versa.

Outside factors, of course, have an influence on current design philosophies.

As roads have improved—become more like tracks—road-racing bikes have become more and more consistently similar to track bikes in their geometry. But there is still a difinitively different breed that is the road bike. Bikes created for criteriums may lean more in the direction of track-bike geometry; those designed for stage racing (which may involve riding more than 150 miles daily for a week or even a month) would tend to lean the other way, but an experienced cyclist knows at a glance that both are designed for road racing.

RATIONAL GEARING

One of the ways a bicycle becomes personalized is that its gearing reflects the capacities and the purposes of its rider—or it *should*. It is amazing to realize how poorly thought out the gearing is on many production bicycles. The fact is that many people—designers and riders alike—never do think about it. The subject is somewhat shrouded in mystique—an absurd situation considering how simple it is.

The track racer is likely to know all he or she needs to know about gearing: *the* gear which suits his or her style best in each particular event. Having only one gear to deal with makes for clear understanding. Most people who ride multiple-geared bicycles learn through experience the *range* of gear ratios that are useful to them in the kind of riding they do; but when it comes to figuring out a rational *system* of ra-

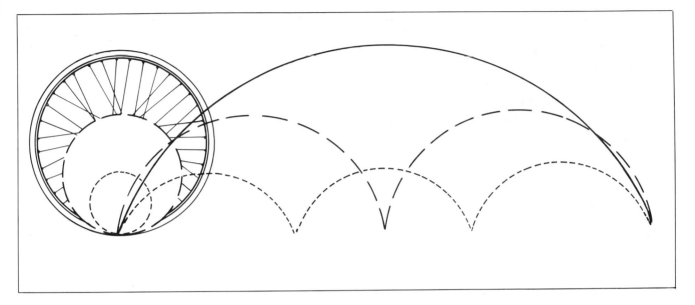

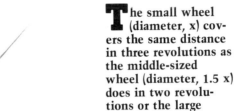

The small wheel (diameter, x) covers the same distance in three revolutions as the middle-sized wheel (diameter, 1.5 x) does in two revolutions or the large wheel (diameter, 3 x) does in one revolution. In other words, the distance covered is directly proportional to the diameter of the wheel.

tios, many people are lost.

The standard multiple-geared high performance bike has ten speeds or, more correctly, ten possible combinations of front chain wheels with rear freewheel cogs. If you go into bicycle shops and actually count the chain wheel and freewheel teeth on the bikes on the floor, you will be amazed to discover how many of these ten-speed machines are, for all practical purposes, five- or six-speed bikes. Careless selection of chain wheels and freewheels can and does lead to *duplication* of gear ratios and to badly distributed ratios as well.

GEAR TALK

Before we get into the question of what gearing is best for your needs, let's make sure we are all speaking the same language. The terminology most commonly used in the United States and Britain originated in the days in which the distance a bike traveled for each revolution of the pedals depended on the diameter (the circumference actually) of the driving wheel. Gearing was introduced for the specific purpose of reducing the size of driving wheels, but the terminology that sprang up related to the size

(diameter) of the wheel as it would be if it *weren't* geared.

A wheel of 30 inches diameter will travel the same distance in two revolutions as a 60-inch wheel will travel in a single revolution; distance traveled is in direct proportion to diameter. So a 30-inch wheel geared at a 2:1 ratio to the pedals (making two revolutions for every revolution of the pedals) has the same *effective* diameter as a 60-inch wheel geared 1:1 (that is, *un*geared). In the gearing parlance, then, a 30-inch wheel geared 2:1 is said to be operating in a "60-inch gear." The same wheel geared 3:1 would

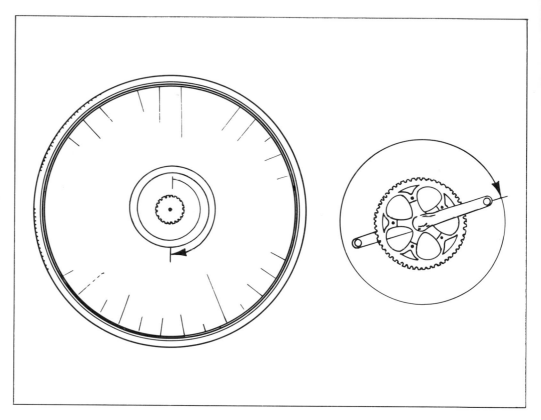

The chain wheel in this diagram has two and one-half times as many teeth as the freewheel cog (chain wheel, 50 T, freewheel, 20 T). For each revolution of the pedals (and chain wheel) the freewheel (and rear wheel) will revolve two and one-half times. In these two and one-half revolutions the 27 inch diameter wheel will travel the same distance (212 inches) as a 67½ inch diameter wheel in one revolution.

be said to be operating in a "90-inch gear."

In a more modern context a setup with the chain running from a front chain wheel of 50 teeth to a rear cog of 20 teeth would be operating in a 67.5-inch gear. Here's how it works. The gear *ratio* is 2.5:1 (50:20 equals 2.5:1). For every one revolution of the pedals, the rear wheel will make 2½ revolutions. It will go 2½ times as far as the same wheel making one revolution; or, in the terms we are using, it would go the same distance as a wheel of 2½ times its diameter making one revolution. The diameter of the standard

bicycle is 27 inches. Twenty-seven times 2½ is 67.5 inches. Clear?

A quick formula for figuring the gearing of your bike is as follows: Divide the number of chain-wheel teeth by the number of teeth on the freewheel cog. Multiply the resulting number by 27, the diameter of the wheel. Gearing (in inches) = $(N_c \div n_f) \times 27$.

It is a rather abstract way to think about gearing, but the terminology has stuck and it is better to understand it than not. The Europeans express gearing in a somewhat more rational way—in terms of the distance the wheel travels per pedal revo-

lution—and maybe that system will be adopted here someday. For now we are stuck with the effective-diameter concept.

IN THE BEGINNING

The first ten-speed gearing systems were designed for racing. The name that has come along, after the fact, to describe them is "half-step" gearing. The reasoning is simple. The freewheel cogs are chosen to produce changes of gearing in increments as nearly equal as possible. The chain wheels are chosen to produce gearing changes of about half the magnitude of

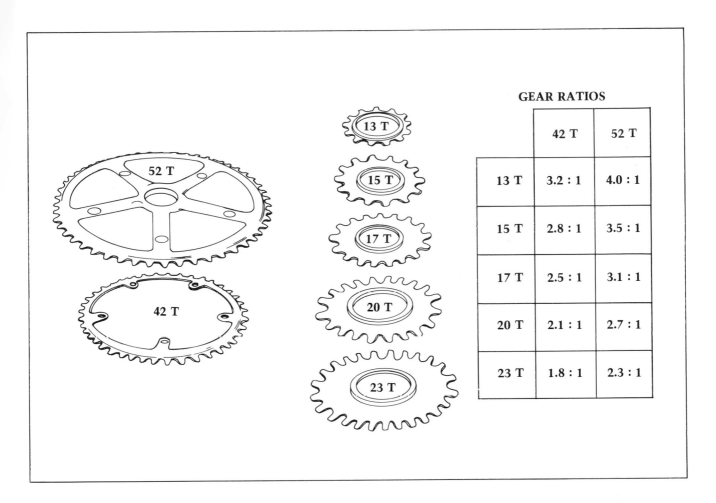

GEAR RATIOS

	42 T	52 T
13 T	3.2 : 1	4.0 : 1
15 T	2.8 : 1	3.5 : 1
17 T	2.5 : 1	3.1 : 1
20 T	2.1 : 1	2.7 : 1
23 T	1.8 : 1	2.3 : 1

Each combination of one chain wheel and one free-wheel sprocket produces a distinct gear ratio between the pedals and the rear wheel. There may be close or exact duplications if gearings are not chosen carefully.

the changes produced by the rear shifts.

My bicycle has classic half-step gearing and can serve as a perfect example. The rear cogs have 15, 17, 19, 21, and 23 teeth respectively, approximating a 12.5 percent increment. The chain wheels are 46 and 49 teeth—almost exactly a 6.25 percent change. The combination gives ten distinct gear ratios, reasonably evenly spaced, between 54 and 88.2 inches. If you were to increase the larger chain wheel by one tooth and reduce the smaller chain wheel by one tooth (giving 45 and 50 teeth) you would get four almost exact duplications within the eight inner combinations, giving a total of six usable speeds.

Half-step gearing eventually fell from favor with racers for two reasons. First, the double shifts necessary to get from one gear to the nearest half-step in some cases

HALF-STEP GEARING

Legend: upper triangle = RATIO, lower triangle = EFFECTIVE GEAR

	15 T	17 T	19 T	21 T	23 T
46 T	3.07 : 1 / 82.8 in.	2.7 : 1 / 73.1 in.	2.42 : 1 / 65.4 in.	2.19 : 1 / 59.1 in.	2.01 : 1 / 54.0 in.
49 T	3.27 : 1 / 88.2 in.	2.88 : 1 / 77.8 in.	2.58 : 1 / 69.6 in.	2.33 : 1 / 63.0 in.	2.13 : 1 / 57.5 in.

CROSSOVER GEARING

	13 T	15 T	17 T	20 T	23 T
44 T	3.38 : 1 / 91.4 in.	2.93 : 1 / 79.2 in.	2.59 : 1 / 69.9 in.	2.20 : 1 / 59.4 in.	1.91 : 1 / 51.6 in.
50 T	3.85 : 1 / 103.8 in.	3.33 : 1 / 90.0 in.	2.94 : 1 / 79.4 in.	2.50 : 1 / 67.5 in.	2.17 : 1 / 58.7 in.

ALPINE GEARING

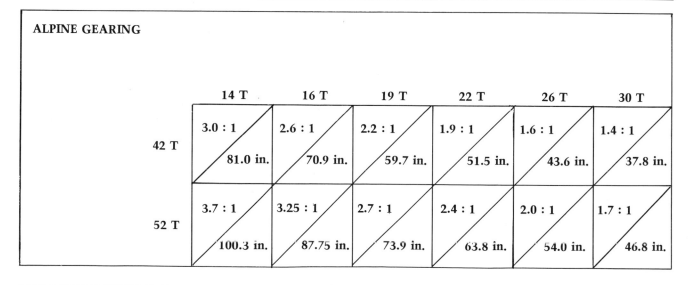

	14 T	16 T	19 T	22 T	26 T	30 T
42 T	3.0 : 1 / 81.0 in.	2.6 : 1 / 70.9 in.	2.2 : 1 / 59.7 in.	1.9 : 1 / 51.5 in.	1.6 : 1 / 43.6 in.	1.4 : 1 / 37.8 in.
52 T	3.7 : 1 / 100.3 in.	3.25 : 1 / 87.75 in.	2.7 : 1 / 73.9 in.	2.4 : 1 / 63.8 in.	2.0 : 1 / 54.0 in.	1.7 : 1 / 46.8 in.

were a hassle. Second, the system didn't offer a very wide *range* of gearing (the 54- to 88-inch range on my bicycle is extremely limited by today's standards). In the interests, then, of efficiency and of expanding gearing range, the "crossover" system was developed. Theoretically, in crossover gearing, the percentage of change in the steps of the rear cluster and the chain wheels are equal. This gives a progression (with a five-speed rear) of six evenly spaced ratios with only one front shift—in the middle. The progression goes (starting on the small chain wheel); biggest rear cog, next rear cog, middle cog, **shift chain wheel,** next rear cog, smallest rear cog. A fairly perfect crossover gearing with changes approximating 15 percent would result from teaming a 13, 15, 17, 20, 23 freewheel with a 44 by 50 front end. The gearing would range from 51.5 to 104 inches in steps of about 10 inches.

FOR MOUNTAIN CLIMBERS

The needs of tourists dictated a different approach to multiple gearing. The system we call alpine gearing was developed to expand the gearing range, primarily in the downward direction (to provide lower gears). The theory calls for evenly spaced steps in the rear cluster and a jump in the chain wheels of 1½ times the rear percentage change. The aim is to provide a good low, a number of evenly spaced middle ratios, and a good high. One combination that works well (with a six-speed rear) is the combination 14, 16, 19, 22, 26, 30 in back, with 42 by 52 in front. This gives a low of 38 inches—not a *low* low, but good enough for many. The high of 100 is high enough for most. Many other combinations are possible, of course, and actual gear selection should always be based on individual capacity. The addition of a third chain wheel offers the possibility of a *much* lower low along with a good range of middle ratios. It should be pointed out here that "fifteen-speed" bike is even more of a misnomer than "ten-speed" usually is. The small chain wheel is *not* intended to provide five new ratios, but one or two at the most. The thing to avoid is the situation in which the middle range of ratios on the larger chain wheels duplicate one another.

CROSS CHAINING

One of the reasons for the development of the crossover and alpine shifting patterns is that the theoretical existence of ten (or fifteen, etc.) gear ratios doesn't jibe very well with physical reality. For the chain to operate efficiently it should be running in a straight line from chain wheel to freewheel. In the combinations that utilized the smallest freewheel cog with the smaller chain wheel and the largest cog with the large chain wheel, the deflection of the chain was extreme enough to cause noticeable problems, especially as the sizes of chain wheels got farther apart. In planning your own personal gearing it is a good idea to keep in mind that extreme cross chaining should be avoided. This means that the extreme combinations noted above should be discounted as theoretically possible gears. Even for those who like neatly placed half-steps, as I do, can do without them at the ends of the spectrum. The crossover system is the most thorough application of this principle. It *is* efficient mechanically, both in terms of chain performance and in the simplicity of the shifting pattern. It is more suited to the needs of racers, though, than alpine or modified half-step gearing.

Much of the energy devoted to improving the bicycle over the past century has taken the form of seeking new or improved materials. The problem has generally been a simple one: find a stronger material or a material of equal strength that is lighter in weight.

NEW HIGH-TECH MATERIALS

The earliest bicycles were made largely of wood and iron. Wood quickly proved to lack the strength necessary for a high performance bicycle building material. Thus, bicycles soon became almost entirely iron machines. As steel making technology developed, iron was increasingly supplanted by steel in bicycle building. (Bicycle building had its impact on the steel industry, too. A number of alloys and some significant manufacturing techniques were developed by experimenters whose primary interest was in bicycle construction.)

The turn-of-the-century bicycle, then,

was built for the most part from steel, rubber, and leather. Only the last of these can be said to be in any sense obsolete. The single most important development in bicycle materials technology since 1900 has been the emergence of aluminum and its alloys as affordable items of commerce. As stronger and stronger

aluminum alloys have been developed, they have been used increasingly to replace steel in the bicycle.

What of plastics, resins, rare metals? These and other exotic substances have been used, but so far their impact has been minimal.

CONVENTIONAL HIGH-TECH

STEEL FRAMES

The vast majority of fine bicycle frames are made from high-grade steel alloys. Other materials *are* being used and the experimentation in this field is one of the developments that we will consider separately. But today (1981) steel remains the material of choice for 99 percent of all frame makers.

The pieces or elements of a bike frame consist of simple shapes—tubes—and complex shapes—the lugs, bottom bracket shell, fork crown, and fork ends or dropouts.

Bicycle tubing constitutes a vast subject in itself. Some of the strongest steel alloys known have been developed specifically for the construction of bicycles. So bike tubing differs from most other kinds of steel tubes, both in the composition of the alloy itself and in the manner in which it is fabricated. A true tube, as opposed to a pipe, is

formed from a solid, pierced ingot of metal, which is drawn over a mandrel (actually a series of mandrels). The morphology of the material never changes; there is no seam or join in a tube. Further, in order to make the tube stronger at the ends (where the tubes are joined to each other and where they are subjected to the most stress) most of the finest bicycle tubes are butted—made thicker by a special manufacturing process.

The great strength of the best bicycle tubing is due to the composition of the alloys used. They contain small but precisely controlled amounts of chromium, molybdenum, manganese, and other trace elements. Different manufacturers use different formulas, but the most common recipe uses chromium and molybdenum and is referred to generically as "chro-mo" or "chrome-moly." The major rival to chrome-moly formulas is the TI Reynolds "531" formula which uses molybdenum and manganese with only a tiny percentage of chromium. The physical properties of these alloys allows tubes to be made with quite thin walls and still retain the strength needed to make a reasonably rigid structure.

Bicycle tube sets are manufactured in standard diameters—top tube, one inch; remaining tubes one-and-a-quarter inch—and in a number of different gauges depending on whether strength or lightness is more important for the particular bicycle in question. All manufacturers make straight gauge tube sets as well as butted. These are the lightest—used only in very special applications where weight reduction is an overriding consideration. Thickness for the standard gauge of first-quality bicycle tubing (not by any means the lightest) runs less than 3/100s of an inch (.0279 inch, to be exact, for the Reynolds 531, in the unbutted section of the tube).

The chemical composition of the steel alloys used in bicycle tubing makes the tubes very strong, but it also makes them very vulnerable to the effects of heat. Since the tubes are joined by brazing—a type of welding in which fairly high heat is used—some of the inherent strength of the material is permanently lost. So the heat must be kept as low as possible. The careless application of too much heat in the brazing process will leave the metal brittle and prone to early and sudden failure under stress. Therefore the skill and care with which assembly is carried out can critically affect the quality of the finished frame.

The manufacture of the parts of the bicycle frame that have complex shapes—the lugs, the bottom bracket shell, the fork crown and the dropouts—takes one of three forms: forging (forming the part out of a solid piece of metal), stamping and welding, or casting. The choice between one method of manufacture and another is often (but certainly not always) a choice dictated by economics. The stamping and welding together of sheet steel

is certainly the least expensive of these processes. Forging and casting are considerably more costly—casting currently being the most expensive method. The casting process used to produce the highest quality bicycle parts is known as investment casting, in which a very accurate wax model of the part is used to make the mold for the actual steel casting. Investment casting techniques allow the production of extremely accurate, finely finished and very detailed parts.

Fork tips or dropouts are either forged or cast. Lugs and bottom bracket shells are made either by the stamp-and-weld method or they are cast. The builders of fine bicycles are turning more and more consistently to cast bottom brackets. They are costly but far superior in strength. There is a trend toward cast lugs, too, but here the stamp-and-weld method does offer some potential advantage to the builder. True custom frame building involves varying the lengths and hence the angles at which the tubes are joined. Cast lugs, while unquestionably strong, are too rigid to be successfully altered in shape, whereas a welded lug can be successfully reshaped to accommodate slight changes of angle. Fork crowns are produced by all three methods, but stamped crowns are rarely if ever found on fine bicycles. As with bottom brackets, the trend is definitely toward casting.

THE LIMITS OF CONVENTIONAL HIGH TECH

Again, most good bicycle frames over the years have been made from steel tubing—from very high-quality steel tubing specially formulated for making bicycle frames. The standard tubings since the mid-1930s have been Reynolds 531 and the various gauges of tubing made by A. L. Columbo. The weight of a lugged frame made from the standard gauge of chrome-molybdenum or manganese-molybdenum alloy tube weighs about 5.5 pounds (2.5 kilograms) with the fork.

In 1977, the Reynolds Company (now called TI Reynolds) came out with another tubing—a radically new formulation they call "753." The new 753 tubing is substantially thinner than tubes made from the 531 formulation or its close relatives. The weight of a frame and fork made from 753 is about 4 pounds (1.8 kilograms). This pound-and-a-half difference is a very significant edge in the world of competition, but the performance of Reynolds 753 would seem to suggest that the limits of steel technology have been reached. While many riders are happy with 753 frames (and the Raleigh team has certainly had notable success riding 753), others note its unacceptable "whippiness." The thinness of the tubing, while making for much appreciated weight saving, diminishes the ability of the material to stand up to stress without flexing. While 753 tubing is *stronger* than 531 and comparable materials, it can never make a *stiffer* frame without being heavier. The reasons for this will be made clear shortly.

The venerable TI Raleigh firm was among the first deemed qualified by equally venerable TI Reynolds to use its new super-light 753 steel alloy tubing.

SEARCHING FOR NEW MATERIALS

Over the decades a number of different materials have been tried out—and most rejected, for one reason or another. An amusing early example was the turn-of-the-century bamboo bicycle. In recent times experimentation with non-standard materials for high-performance bicycle frames has concentrated on aluminum alloys, on titanium, and on various fiber-resin compounds. Hard aluminum alloys have been around for decades in various forms. Titanium has been around, but it took the technological demands of the space program to make it enough of an "item of commerce" to lower the price sufficiently so that it could be *considered* as a viable frame-building material. It is still very expensive. Carbon (graphite) and boron fibers are also products of space-age technology. They are the most recent arrivals on the list.

The aim in considering any new material for frame building is to arrive at a result that has the same properties as a steel frame but is lighter. Right? Well, not really. The objective is to make a *better* frame, whatever that may happen to be.

What do we wish a "good" frame to provide? The question seems a reasonable point of departure. In addition to lightness, which is always desirable, we want a bicycle frame to be strong. There are different kinds of materials strengths, however. We want a bike frame to be rigid and durable. We want it to resist torsion and compression (if it twists or bends in use, valuable pedaling force is wasted) and we want it to be unbreakable (a broken frame can't be ridden at all, regardless of what physical properties it may have). We also would like our frame to be comfortable to ride. Most bicycles are ridden over rough surfaces, and a great deal of road shock may be transmitted through the frame to the rider depending on the material from which the frame is made as well as the tube angles.

PHYSICAL PROPERTIES

In order to get a clearer picture of the nature of the balancing act that is involved in choosing frame-building materials, we will have to consider some more precise definitions of the properties of materials—definitions made by physicists. The whole game revolves around a key term: elasticity. Elasticity is the ability of a material to respond to encountering a force by changing shape. The measure of elasticity of any given material is called its "modulus of elasticity." It tells us how much force is required to produce a given amount of deformation (or, conversely, how much deformation will result from the application of a given amount of force—these are exactly the same).

Another measure of elasticity that has significance in this discussion is the point past which the material cannot be stretched (deformed) and still return to its original shape. This point is known as the "elastic limit." When a material has been subjected to enough force that its elastic limits have been surpassed, it becomes permanently deformed (*bent* is a good synonym) *and* permanently weakened. Finally, the "ultimate" or "breaking" strength of a material is the measure of the amount of force that will result in the material failing altogether or fracturing.

Just to keep the remainder of the discussion simple, now that we have looked at the precise terminology we will refer to the

The Vector 'Beta', the first human powered land vehicle (in the single-rider category) to exceed the speed of 55 mph. Other multi-rider Vectors produced by the same design team have traveled in excess of 62 mph.

This is a detail of the unconventional, under-the-leg position of the indirect steering system and other controls.

The Avatar 2000: the first well-engineered, high-quality recumbent cycle to reach the American market. The Avatar's long wheelbase, low center of gravity, and stretched-out riding position combine to make it safer, more efficient, and more comfortable than conventional "upright" bikes.

The Klein 'Stage' bicycle: the bike that redefined the terms "racing design" and "touring design." Held to be unsurpassed for both touring and long-distance road racing, it is not only efficient (strong, stiff) but stable and comfortable to ride. The unusual combination of attributes results from unusual materials and unique design principles.

A colorful entry in the 1978 IHPVA Speed Championships by Alec Brooks. It logged a top speed of 43.78 mph to capture 6th place among single-rider vehicles.

This prone-supine tandem entry by Phil and Sue Norton, veterans of several seasons of competition in the Speed Championships, managed a top speed of 56.56 mph and a 3rd place finish in the 1979 time trials.

Raleigh was one
of the first
builders licensed to
use Reynolds' revolu-
tionary new super-
light steel tubing,
known as "753." The
result of the Reynolds/
Raleigh collaboration
is this frame, the Ra-
leigh Team 753, used
with considerable suc-
cess by the Raleigh-
sponsored racing
team.

The Graftek is one of the few fiber-composite frames that ever went beyond the experimental stage. Frame tubes were graphite filaments bonded over thin aluminum tubes in various winding patterns, depending on the specific stresses each frame member is subjected to in use. After a brief but intense ad campaign and a period in which the frames were used in competition by notable American racers, Exxon took the Graftek of the market.

The one extant, available titanium bike frame: the British Speedwell. Probably the lightest single frame around, weighing in at about 3.75 pounds, the Speedwell has found favor with tourists as well as racers.

The Motobecane 'Prolight,' otherwise known as the Vitus 'Supercadre'—a new production aluminium alloy frame featuring tubes of considerable thickness (in comparison to steel) glued around specially cast and machined lugs, dropouts, and fork crown.

property described by the modulus of elasticity (i.e., how *much* bending will take place per unit of force) as "stiffness," and the properties that have to do with elastic limit and breaking strength (i.e., how much force will result in permanent damage to the material) as "strength."

MATERIALS COMPARISONS

In order to make meaningful comparisons between the properties of any two materials, the properties in question must be related to some other factor. In engineering terms that basis of comparison is often weight (technical-

ly, density). In other words one material can be said to have more or less stiffness *in relation to its weight* than another. The relationships are generally expressed in terms of a ratio—a stiffness-to-weight ratio or a strength-to-weight ratio.

Elasticity Considered

Each of the elements has a constant modulus of elasticity. All steels, for example, have a modulus of approximately 30 million pounds per square inch (meaning that a one-pound force applied to a cube of steel one-inch tall would compress it one thirty-millionth of an inch). Likewise all aluminum alloys have the

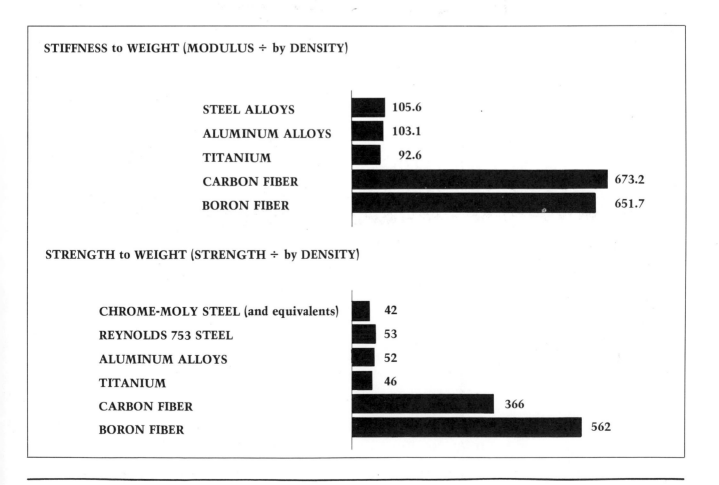

STIFFNESS to WEIGHT (MODULUS ÷ by DENSITY)

STEEL ALLOYS	105.6
ALUMINUM ALLOYS	103.1
TITANIUM	92.6
CARBON FIBER	673.2
BORON FIBER	651.7

STRENGTH to WEIGHT (STRENGTH ÷ by DENSITY)

CHROME-MOLY STEEL (and equivalents)	42
REYNOLDS 753 STEEL	53
ALUMINUM ALLOYS	52
TITANIUM	46
CARBON FIBER	366
BORON FIBER	562

same modulus regardless of the specific composition of the alloy, and the same holds true for the remaining materials.

Aluminum alloys have a modulus about one-third as great as steel (about 10 million psi). Titanium is better, nearly half as stiff. Carbon and boron fibers have a modulus of elasticity just about twice that of steel (60 million psi).

On a *stiffness-to-weight* basis, however, things look a bit different. Amazingly steel, aluminum, and titanium come out quite close to one another—steel and aluminum very close indeed. Titanium has a slightly lower stiffness-to-weight ratio. The fibers, on the other hand, are approximately six times as stiff per unit weight as steel and aluminum—an impressive and intriguing figure.

Strength Considered

While elasticity is given and constant for each of the elements, its strength is influenced by a number of possible factors. In the case of "coherent" materials, such as the metals, the composition of mixtures or alloys greatly determines strength. In the case of the fibers, which are not coherent, the material strength is related to how they were bonded together. Purely physical factors can also have an influence.

Rough figures for the breaking strengths of the strongest steel alloys run between 120,000 and 150,000 pounds per square inch. The tougher aluminum alloys run in the vicinity of 50,000 psi and titanium around 75,000 psi. The carbon fibers have strengths ranging between 200,000 and 300,000 psi, while boron fibers have a breaking strength of approximately 500,000 psi.

On a *strength-to-weight* basis the metals, again, all fall within a close range. The strongest aluminum alloys and the strongest steel alloy (Reynolds 753) are almost identical. Titanium and the more common

chrome-molybdenum and manganese-molybdenum alloys are also close to each other, with titanium having a slight edge. Carbon fibers have a strength-to-weight ratio roughly ten times as great as the standard chrome-moly steels, and boron fibers are still stronger, about ten times the strength-to-weight of the best steel and aluminum alloys. To say the very least these fiber or filament materials suggest staggering future possibilities.

EFFECTS OF HEAT

So far, on the face of it, the various metals would seem to have little to recommend one over another, but the whole story is not in yet. Steel and aluminum alloys are weakened by heat. Since brazing and "silver soldering" are the only methods used to join steel tubes in bike building, some weakening of the tubing is bound to occur in the frame-building process. (Reynolds 753 is particularly sensitive to this problem because of its chemical composition and its extremely thin gauge. For this reason the manufacturer exercises extensive control over the building process, allowing only the lower-heat silver-soldering process to be used with 753 tubing.) Careless brazing can seriously weaken a steel frame, but with careful work the strength losses in high-quality steel-alloy frames are held to be acceptable. Is there any choice, after all?

Aluminum alloys are also significantly weakened by heat. This has suggested to many that welding is an unacceptable method of joining aluminum tubes in cycle frame making. Numerous other methods of joining have been tried with aluminum materials. It has been long known, however, that the material recovered some portion of its lost strength simply through the aging process. Careful heat treatment is also effective (ironically) in restoring strength lost to welding-temperature heat. According to one builder, Gary Klein, the total strength of aluminum can be restored by heat treatment.

Titanium does not suffer significant weakening as a result of the welding process.

TUBING DESIGN

Aside from the effects of heat the form of the members used in construction affects the overall strength and rigidity of the material. Virtually all bicycle frames (up until the last couple of years) have been made from round tubes. The sizes of these tubes have been standardized for decades. The outside diameter of the standard seat and down tubes is 1⅛ inches (28.6 millimeters). The standard top tube is one inch (25.4 millimeters) in diameter. Head tubes are approximately 1¼ inches (31.75 millimeters) across. Most experiments in bicycle-tube production have accepted these standards as a starting point and have thereby failed to take possible advantage of changing tube dimensions other than gauge. The general idea has been to make the tube as thin as is consistent with adequate structural integrity—using those tube diameters.

Here we get to a very important point—its significance cannot be overemphasized. There is nothing sacred about the standard tube diameters. When the diameter of a tube is changed, *its effective stiffness and strength change too.* Strength increases in direct proportion to the increase in diameter; stiffness increases in proportion to the square of the diameter. That is to say, for a given wall thickness (gauge), if you make the tube larger in diameter, you make it stronger and considerably stiffer. It is more resistant to both torsion (twisting) and compression (bending). (Of course it also gets heavier, but we'll get back to that.)

There is a limit to the possibility of increasing tube strength by enlarging the diameter; there is a point at which the thickness of the tube wall becomes insufficient to stand up to stress. Engineers estimate this point for most materials at a wall thickness equal to one-fiftieth of the total tube diameter. Thicker walls represent a safety factor; thinner walls would be prone to buckling.

The average thickness of the tube walls in a standard double-butted tube of the Reynolds 531 variety is around one forty-fifth of the tube diameter—a safe figure. In Reynolds 753 and some other superlight tubes wall thickness is a potentially hazardous one fifty-fifth or so of tube diameter.

So—enlarging tube diameter makes it stiffer and stronger. Making the tube walls thicker (while the diameter remains constant) does the same, although the increase is less weight efficient (there is a smaller gain in strength and stiffness per unit weight gain). Both these principles have been put into practice (as well as a combination of the two) in making up for the inherent deficiencies in the ''absolute'' strength and stiffness of the lighter materials in comparison with steel. The key to practical solutions has been in experimenting with *both* variables, finding the optimal combination of tube diameter and gauge that allows either a significant weight advantage with comparable structural integrity or comparable weight with greater structural integrity (or possibly a compromise/combination of advantages).

ALUMINUM ALLOY FRAMES

Experimentation in the building of aluminum frames has been in progress—off and on—since the turn of the century. As of this writing there are but two aluminum frames *on the market* that have met with any measure of acceptance and success. (A third has appeared recently and is in the early stages of marketing.)

THE ALAN FRAME

Strong aluminum-alloy tubes have been around for a long time. What has hung people up was the problem of joining them together without sowing the seeds of their own destruction. Not only are aluminum alloys weakened by heat, as noted already, they are also very much prone to sudden failure—especially along convenient "fracture planes" such as those provided by cuts, nicks, and scratches.

The Italian designer and entrepreneur Falconi spent five years working out the bugs in his aluminum production frame, which has now been on the market for a number of years and is in considerable demand in certain racing circles. The frame is marketed here under the name Alan (*al*uminum, *an*odized). The Alan frame is designed around a tube that is quite thick in comparison with standard butted alloy-steel tubes: two millimeters (.079 inches) in comparison with .625 millimeters (.024 inches) for the unbutted portion of a standard gauge of Reynolds 531 tube—or more than *three times* the thickness! The lugs and the bottom-bracket shell are cast and machined (also out of aluminum alloy). As-

sembly techniques involve threading, gluing and the use of set screws. Unlike most other aluminum frame sets (including the ones that have never reached the production stage), the Alan uses aluminum fork blades and crown. In the heavier model, the 2.25 kilogram (4.95 pound) "Competizione," the steering tube is of steel. In the 2.09 kilo (4.6 pound) "Super" model, even the steerer is of aluminum.

The tubing used on the Alan frame is evidently no exception to the rule of nicks and scratches breeding broken frames. The manufacturer recommends cushioning any areas of expected abrasion with tape. One wonders how the threading of tube ends avoids creating the same problems. Presumably, however, that has been dealt with. One of the advantages of the cemented-assembly technique (assuming that the bonding is of adequate strength) is that the cemented joints should help to reduce overall shock transmission markedly.

As a matter of practical overall engineering policy, Signor Falconi elected to make all the Alan frames with the same frame angles. The casting of lugs with different angles for every different frame size would indeed have been expensive. In any case, regardless of frame size, all Alan frames do have the same frame tube angles, the same bottom-bracket height, the same chain-stay length and the same fork rake.

THE KLEIN BICYCLE

The other successful aluminum frame is a very different animal. It had its genesis in a

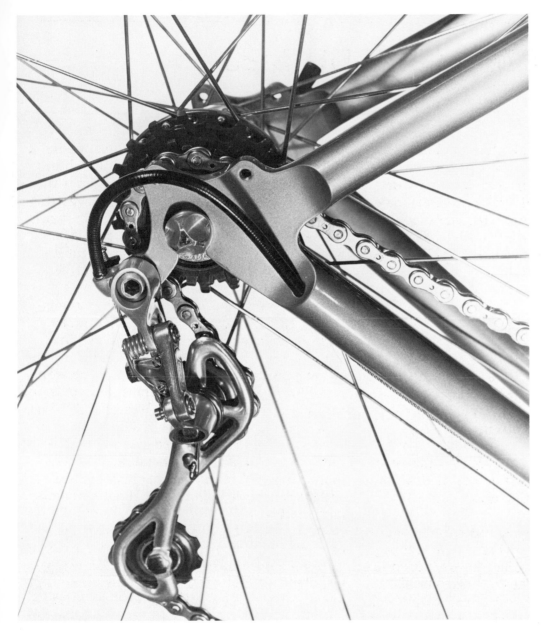

The Klein frame is unusual even in its details. Almost no part of the frame or fork is a standard component supplied by another manufacturer. Quality of detail and finish is uniform throughout.

special study group of students at the Massachusetts Institute of Technology. The objective of the project, under the guidance of Professor Shawn Buckley, was to improve on the performance of the standard steel bike frame—that is to make a *better* frame out of whatever it took. After reviewing the physical and mechanical properties of a number of materials, the group decided to cast its lot with

the possibilities inherent in aluminum. From this beginning the Klein Company emerged three years later.

Gary Klein, who followed up his earliest work with constant reevaluation, experimentation and exhaustive engineering analysis, has developed a bicycle tubing that utilizes the structural properties of aluminum alloys to their best advantage. The key to the

The sleek appearance of Klein aluminum alloy bicycle frames results from carefully executed, lugless welded construction and impeccable finishing techniques.

success of Klein's frames is the tubing diameter. Willing to turn his back on tradition and seek the most efficient combination of elements, Klein ultimately elected to build his frames out of 1¼- and 1½-inch tubes with a wall thickness of about .05 inches (roughly double the thickness of a typical Reynolds 531 tube). The result is a frame that is lighter than a Reynolds 531 frame, marginally heavier than a Reynolds 753 frame, but stronger and much stiffer than either.

Klein frames are carefully mitered and welded by the tungsten/inert-gas method. No lugs are used; the joints are carefully built up and filleted. After welding the frame undergoes careful and extensive heat treatment. According to Klein, "the heat-treating process causes the grain structures of the alloy to

flow into a uniform, unbroken pattern throughout the entire frame. This completely relieves welding stresses, creates the highest possible temper condition of the alloy, and increases its hardness, fatigue resistance and yield [breaking] strength."

Another Klein specialty is laminating boron reinforcements onto the chain stays, the seat stays, and the fork blades. The boron fiber adds substantially to the stiffness of these frame members whose structural configuration doesn't make them particularly efficient at resisting lateral stresses, making up for that deficiency in large part. As if that weren't enough, the boron fiber laminations provide a considerable degree of vibration damping, improving the ride and feel of the bicycle significantly.

Klein attributes his success to one thing above all else: the willingness to work out all the design features thoroughly—to solving all the engineering problems—before offering his product to the public. This attitude bespeaks conscientiousness. It also takes courage to pursue the development of a product that aims at making a substantial improvement over existing standards *whatever the cost.* These words are used advisedly. Klein bicycles are expensive—very expensive. There are two basic designs: a criterium-style bicycle with high bottom bracket and short wheelbase; and a "stage" model with a longer wheelbase, longer top tube, and lower bottom bracket, suitable for general road racing and touring. The price? Variable, from just under $3,500 to just under $4,000. There are also special models available at substantially higher cost. The cost is high, yes, but there is a market for the product—and I have yet to hear anyone disagree with the proposition that, all things being equal, these are the finest bicycles available.

Klein plans to continue improving his bicycles. He is not particularly wedded to any one notion of what a bicycle should be or should be made of. As yet Klein uses steel forks in his frame sets. He feels the stress on the steering tube is so great that only steel will do a satisfactory job—according to Klein's standards. So far he has not worked out a satisfactory solution to the problem of fastening a steel steerer to an aluminum fork—satisfactory, that is, to him.

THE VITUS SUPERCADRE

The third aluminum frame, mentioned parenthetically at the beginning of this discussion,

has been made available only recently. It is made (or marketed) under the Vitus marque. (Vitus is the trade name of bicycle tubing manufactured by the French firm *Ateliers de la Rive.*) The aluminum alloy tubing is called Vitus Duralinox 979.

The Vitus frame, which bears the name "Supercadre" ("superframe"), bears more resemblance to the Alan than to the Klein—much more. Made from what appears to be slightly larger than standard tubing, the Supercadre is assembled by cementing the tubes to the specially cast and machined lugs and bottom-bracket shell. The lugs, bottom bracket, and dropouts are made with flanges that fit *inside* the various tubes. Cementing, according to the manufacturer's literature, is carried out under the strictest control, using the latest aircraft adhesives and the impeccable techniques necessary to make them work properly. As with the Alan frame the cementing of the parts should make for a frame with excellent vibration-damping characteristics.

Forks on the Vitus frames are made entirely from Duralinox 979, including the steering tube. All of the fork components are cemented to a specially designed cast crown. One interesting innovation on the Vitus frame is that the head tube and the lugs that would, in a conventional bicycle, connect it to the top and down tubes, have been incorporated into a single casting. That's right—the Supercadre has a one-piece head tube with the top tube and down-tube lugs built right in.

Like the Alan the Supercadre comes in a range of frame sizes—from 49 to 60 centimeters (19¼ to 23½ inches)—but a number of the dimensions are standard on all sizes—namely, head angle, chain-stay length, bottom-bracket height, and fork rake (although a fork with a 5-centimeter rake is available as a special option in place of the standard fork, which has a 4-centimeter rake). Weights for

the finished frames with fork are reported to run from 1.72 kilograms (3.8 pounds) for the 49-centimeter size to 1.89 kilos (4.2 pounds) for the 60-centimeter size, making them lighter than anything but titanium.

Interestingly, despite its short tenure on the bicycle scene, the Vitus Supercadre is already being used on a stock bicycle—the "Prolight" by Motobecane, also a French firm. (The French like to stick together.)

A specially cast head tube and fork crown simplify potential problems of construction in the new glued-together Vitus aluminum alloy frame from France.

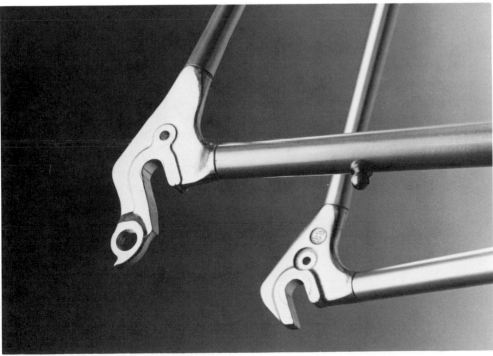

D ropouts on the Vitus 'Supercadre' are also cast—like the rest of the lugs—with tangs that fit inside the frame tubes. All frame angles are predetermined by the lug configurations.

TITANIUM FRAMES

The potential of titanium as a frame-building material has been recognized for a long time, at least since the mid-1950s when the first prototypes were built and exhibited, but it wasn't until 1972 that a titanium frame was actually put into production and marketed (by the Speedwell Gear Co., England).

As we have seen, titanium has a modulus of elasticity about one-half that of steel (it is half as stiff). Its breaking strength is about 40 percent lower. Its weight or density is also just about 40 percent lower than that of steel. In stiffness-to-weight and strength-to-weight terms, it is comparable to steel, though slightly inferior in both categories. But we also saw that by altering either the diameter or the gauge of the tubing (or both) that it was possible to outperform standard steel tubing and still stay under its weight, or at least to keep the weights comparable.

The early Speedwell frames were not very successful from this point of view. They have been described as simple copies of standard steel frames in titanium. They were very light (about 3.5 pounds) but very "dead" to ride. Unfortunately they seem to have given titanium a bad name. They set the tone for much of the popular wisdom that has condemned titanium as a frame-building material ever since.

Speedwell has been criticized as having been too eager to get their frames on the market, not waiting for the engineering to be worked out thoroughly. This is, I think, a valid criticism. The Speedwell frame has undergone considerable redesign over the ensuing years with the result that many of the original objections have been removed.

Other manufacturers were somewhat more cautious about launching their efforts. The Titan, produced under the aegis of a division of the Teledyne Corporation, was one such effort. The Titan used somewhat larger-than-standard tubes (1⅛ inch diameter), and it employed a titanium alloy with considerably higher tensile strength than the pure or almost pure metal used by Speedwell. The Titan also used internal liners at critical points for added strength.

The Titan earned a mixed reputation. Some say that, though it was the product of virtually unlimited technical resources (Teledyne), it was not fully worked out from an engineering point of view—too much emphasis was placed on keeping the weight to a minimum without regard for structural integrity and durability. Others describe it as having been a sophisticated and successful frame.

In any case the past tense is used here, since the Teledyne Titan is only a memory—the frame went out of production several years ago. One of the factors in its failure to catch on was certainly its price. It came onto the market at a roughly double the cost of a fine steel frame. The other factor seems to be that it did not succeed in demonstrating a clear advantage over steel frames. At least it was not enough of a money maker for a big corporation like Teledyne, and so it has passed into oblivion.

As mentioned, Speedwell is still producing frames, much improved over the originals. It is an amazing experience to pick up one of these feather-light objects—it just

The Speedwell titanium frame— probably the lightest frame around, but not the stiffest. Note the lugless, welded construction.

doesn't seem *possible.* It does strike me, however, that the fact that I see very few of them on the road (i.e., very few choose to race them) is a clear indication that there is more to a frame than the weight that isn't there, if you see what I mean.

FIBER-COMPOSITE FRAMES

Graphite and boron fibers are certainly the most intriguing potential frame-building materials around. (I say potential, for it has yet to be conclusively demonstrated that they can be used with real success.) The numbers suggest that they should be capable of far outstripping steel—at twice the stiffness and four times the strength per unit weight. Well, that just goes to show that numbers don't tell the whole story.

Steel has some properties that these wonder materials don't have—and they could use them. One of these properties is coherence. Metals, by nature, "hang together." Fibers, unfortunately, do not. They must be glued together or embedded in some other material in order to become a building material. Then again joining steel tubes (metal tubes in general) is simple—aside from questions of the effects of heat. There is no method of joining fiber tubes that offers comparable integrity.

So the first necessity is that a way be found to make the fibers or filaments into tubes (at least in terms of most of the thinking that has gone into the problem so far). The materials that have been used for this purpose are epoxy and polyester resins. The fibers are embedded in the resins with particular winding patterns that maximize resistance to particular stresses (one of the major theoretical advantages of the material to begin

with). That's a plus. A minus is that since the tubes are an amalgam of two different, unrelated materials with decidedly different physical properties, they behave in unpredictable ways in response to stress—non-linear, engi-

Graphite fibers are wound differently in different parts of the Graftek frame in order to cope with different stresses. The differences in the winding pattern in the fork blades and the down tube are clearly visible in this photograph.

One of the few fiber-composite frames ever to make it to the marketplace, the Graftek used graphite-over-aluminum tubes cemented into substantial cast lugs. It made a viable frame but, apparently, one that lacked that special edge of performance.

neers call it.

Perhaps the major stumbling block to the successful use of fiber-composite tubes in frame building, however, has been that the tubes are hard to join together effectively. The only solutions that have been tried with anything like success have been gluing, or clamping *and* gluing the various tubes into metal lugs, etc. None of these seem to have worked —well enough. It is possible that the cementing techniques now being used on the Vitus frames will prove to be the salvation of fiber-composites.

We'll have to wait and see, however. Today there is not one single fiber tube frame on the market. There *have been* a number of well-backed attempts to come up with a viable graphite filament frame, but none has stood the test of time. The Composite Development "Graphite U.S.A." used epoxy-graphite tubes glued into aluminum lugs. The Composite Sports "Line Seeker" took a somewhat different approach, laminating the graphite fibers over aluminum tubes, which were then fastened in steel lugs. The only fiber frame to ever go into major production was the Graftek, another graphite over-alumi-

num composite, marketed by a division of the Exxon Corporation. The Graftek was given a lot of promotion and some notable U.S. racers (most notably the Stetina brothers and John Howard) raced on the frames for a while, but there wasn't enough interest (or profit) to continue the process of working out design problems.

So the tantalizing notion of materials that are "stronger than steel" still dangles there in technological space. It may well be that carbon and boron fibers do not, in reality, have the potential to be used as primary structural materials in bicycle building. On the other hand it may simply be that no one has yet come up with the vital concept that will make it work. (If we look back once again to the situation as it was 100 years ago when many people were striving to find solutions to basic problems of bicycle building, we are reminded that answers are sometimes slow in coming, regardless of the zeal of the seekers.)

In any case, what is certain is that no one has managed so far to turn these technological miracle materials into a practical or a *commercial* success.

All of the preceding relates to attempts at improving the bicycle by finding new materials that will make it lighter or stronger—or both. Not one of the frames discussed involved any significant deviation from the conventional form of the frame. They vary within the design limitations discussed in the Anatomy section in the sense that some are criterium-style designs as opposed to general road racing designs and so forth, but that is as far as it goes.

THE SHAPE OF BIKES TO COME

This streamlined tandem, entered by designer R. Trout in the 1977 IHPVA Speed Championships, typified the early airplanc-wing dc signs. The best time recorded by this vehicle was just short of 35 mph.

Changing the admittedly efficient and refined "diamond" configuration in the bicycle seems to be the also-chosen line of approach to the problem of improvement, at least in the realm of high-performance bicycles for adults. Very little has been tried in the way of fundamental design change.

RIGI BICI-CORTA

One of the few different bicycle designs that *has* appeared, the work of Italian industrialist Giorgio Rinaldi, is the Ri-Gi (*Ri*naldi, *Gi*orgio) "Bici-Corta." The "short bicycle" has one interesting deviation from standard design: the seat tube as been replaced by divided, twin tubes, each about the size of the seat stays on an ordinary bicycle. The result of this change is that the wheelbase can now be made considerably shorter than was ever possible in a conventional design. The presence of the seat tube was always the limiting factor in shortening wheelbase. Signor Rinaldi figured out a way to do away with that limitation. The rear wheel of his bicycles runs *between* the twin tubes.

According to the designer, the following benefits result from this new design feature: reduced weight (shorter chain and seat stays), increased lateral stiffness (due largely to the position of the twin seat tubes' attachment to the bottom-bracket shell), improved overall acceleration and hill-climbing ability, and greater maneuverability. The end product is a bicycle with a chain-stay length of 14¾ inches, a full 1¼ inches shorter than the generally accepted lower limit of 16 inches. Total wheelbase is 36½ inches, about 1½ inches shorter than even the most radical designs of other builders. The tube angles are extremely steep: head tube angle 77° for both road and track models, seat tube for the road bike is 79° and for the track model, 78°.

The Bici-Corta is an interesting example of an idea carried far in the direction of its logical conclusion (at the risk of arriving at an unwieldy result). While these bicycles should, theoretically, be unsurpassed in sprinting and hill climbing, by the same theory they should also be uncomfortable to ride and difficult to handle. Reports have borne this out, though individual conclusions have been mixed regarding whether it is still worth the effort.

My comments on the conservatism of bike racers notwithstanding, several racing teams, including the Polish National Team, have embraced the Bici-Corta with enthusiasm. Results so far have not demonstrated any conclusive advantage to its use in typical road-racing situations.

A final note: Not all that is unfamiliar is new. The short wheel-base bike with a twin seat-tube arrangement was first tried in the 1930s by the Saxon Bicycle Company.

THE RECUMBENT CYCLE

If you keep up with bicycle magazines or engineering magazines—or even with the Sunday supplements of major metropolitan newspapers— the chances are pretty good that you have heard of the recumbent bicycle: the bicycle you ride sitting (or lying) down. The chances are less that you have actually seen one in the flesh. While they have created quite a stir in the public eye in the last few years, there are very, very few around—on the streets at least.

Well, you are saying to yourself, we have finally gotten around to something that really *is* new. Wrong again, I'm afraid. The fact is that the first recumbent bicycle produced was the French Velocar, introduced in 1933. The Velocar was certainly an eye-opener in its day. The recumbent machine promptly began breaking speed records and beating every other bicycle in sight. So, shall we say, alarming was its impact on the racing scene that it was peremptorily banned from any official competition. There was a touring model Velocar, too, and quite a sophisticated machine it was, but its strangeness apparently had an off-putting effect on the public.

THE AVATAR 2000

When Professor David G. Wilson of M.I.T. established a prize for developments in "human-powered land transportation" in the late 1960s, however, the memory of the Velocar proved to be very much alive. Several of the designs submitted were of the recumbent bicycle type. Dr. Wilson was intrigued by this line of thinking and pursued it over the succeeding years. His first collaboration with a bicycle builder, Fred Willkie of California, produced a workable prototype. Further collaboration with Massachusetts builders Richard Forrestal and Harold Maciejewski eventually produced the Avatar 2000™, a hand-built production recumbent bicycle, and Fomac, Inc., a company to produce the machines.

The advantages of the recumbent design center around its more efficient utilization of the power available in the human engine. A rider in a more or less horizontal position, with support behind the back, can easily generate 50 to 60 percent more power in pedaling than seated atop a conventional bicycle. This means riding faster or riding farther on the same expenditure of energy. (You can easily verify this for yourself. Sit on the floor and try pushing some heavy object with your feet. Now sit with your back against a wall and try pushing again. You can feel there is much more force behind your kick in the second instance. You can *measure* the difference if you have a bathroom scale handy.)

This then is the basic innovation—putting the body in line with the direction of leg push brings much more of the musculature into play in pedaling. But there are other advantages in the recumbent design as well. The lower profile markedly diminishes wind resistance, one of the major factors in cycling effort. Recumbents are safer in many ways, too. Their center of gravity is much lower, making for greater overall stability. Further, the rider is

The Avatar 2000 recumbent bicycle may well prove to be the beginning of a revolution in the shape of bicycles for the layman.

much closer to the ground so, in case of an upset, there is much less distance to fall and the reclining position virtually eliminates the possibility of "headers." As Avatar's designers put it, "In the event of a spill, one tends to land on one's feet, not on the face or head." Add to this, greatly increased comfort for the rider (the seat is like an armchair and none of the rider's weight is resting on the rider's hands, arms, or shoulders as with the conventional bicycle), and a more favorable position of the upper body for breathing purposes and you have something that not only looks very different, it *is* different in very significant ways.

Fomac, Inc., has been turning out the Avatar 2000 for a relatively short time. Numbers will be fairly limited—750 units were built in the first year of go-ahead production, with 1,000 slated for the following year. The machine is built from a combination of Reynolds 532 tubes (including the shortened fork) and type 4130 chrome-molybdenum tubes for the structural frame members and two types of aluminum alloy tubing for the seat, handlebars, etc. (Despite the use of these lightweight materials, the finished bicycle weighs in at a rather hefty 29 pounds. Further lightening of the machine would seem to be an

early objective in its future development.) The front wheel is small (16 inches in diameter); the back wheel a standard 27-incher. The components are first-class. Overall they are fine, lovingly made machines. The price (about $2,000 at this time) reflects that.

The appearance of the Avatar was eagerly awaited and much of the early production was spoken for long before the finished bicycles began to emerge from the workshops. Solid commercial success for this innovative bicycle would certainly go a long way toward encouraging further "radical" design ideas on the public.

OTHER RECUMBENTS

Within less than a year after the Avatar's arrival on the scene, two more recumbent bicycles have appeared on the market, both on the West Coast.

The Easy Racer, designed by Gardner Martin, is in many ways similar to the Avatar. This is not to suggest that it is in any sense a copy. It simply shares some of the more salient design features such as the long wheelbase, a small front wheel, and weight distribution favoring the rear

wheel. It is made of similar materials and sells at a similar price.

One of the most noticeable differences is in the steering system. In contrast to the Avatar's indirect, linked, under-the-leg steering, the Easy Racer uses a direct, conventional system—or as close to conventional as is compatible with the long contour of the bike. The steeply slanted head angle, heavily raked fork, and backswept handlebars apparently combine for very responsive handling.

Another difference is that the Easy Racer was truly developed as a racing machine. Martin designed originally to compete in the IHPVA Speed Championships (see pages 185 to 189) where he and it had considerable success. The commercial model lacks the full teardrop fairing of the competition model but does employ the Zzipper fairing (see page 189).

The Easy Racer is a thoroughly worked out and tested machine. Its performance credentials are beyond reproach. At this stage designer-manufacturer Martin is in the process of trying to find ways to fill a demand that far outstrips his production capacity. That, I am sure, will change.

The other Californian entry into the recumbent field is a machine called the

Hyper-Cycle. The Hyper-Cycle is definitely aiming for a different segment of the market. The finished bicycle sells for under $400, and a kit version is available for substantially less. Early reports on the Hyper-Cycle indicate that there are some bugs still to be worked out, but the same can be said about quite a number of the more experimental machines that have come on the market, past and present. The availability of an affordable recumbent will, at the very least, give many people an opportunity to try out the recumbent idea and judge for themselves its merits and possibilities.

DRIVETRAIN INNOVATIONS

The pedal–crank–chain wheel drive configuration is one of the features of the bicycle that has escaped the scrutiny of designers and improvers, or so one might judge from the similarity of today's available bicycles to those produced ninety years ago. Chain wheels have been made lighter, but they differ in no fundamental way from those on bikes of the 1890s. Multiple gearing has brought into being multiple chain wheels, but the functional operation of each is identical with the single chain wheel on any turn-of-the-century bicycle. A natural inference would be that the possibility of improvement, change, innovation, or whatever we choose to call it, was absent—that perfection had been attained at the outset in the utter simplicity of the circular chain wheel.

Contrary to the evidence, however—or, rather, in spite of the lack of *visible* evidence—a number of bicycle theorists and designers have devoted serious thought over several decades to the nagging and undeniable fact that the natural mechanical motion of the human leg does not "interface" particularly efficiently with the circular motion of bicycle cranks. Obviously the motion of the legs can be reconciled to the motion of the pedals with a fair degree of effectiveness, but it is far from being a perfectly efficient adaptation.

Prior to the development of the safety bicycle, there were a number of drive mechanisms that bore little resemblance to anything we are familiar with today. Macmillan's treadle-driven cycle and the American "Star" are two interesting examples. But once the safety bike had reached its standard form in the late 1880s it took a long time for attention to focus on the efficiency of the chain drive. The earliest known attempt to attack the leg–chain wheel interface problem came in the 1930s with the development of a very simple improvement: an oval chain wheel. What the oval chain wheel did was to create, in effect, a continually fluctuating gear ratio, coordinating the increase and decrease in effective gearing with the various phases of the leg motion in pedaling. The fatter part of the chain wheel created a higher gear during the downward push of the leg; the narrower segment reduced the ratio during the in-between part of the pedaling cycle. The timing of the rise and fall in effective gearing could be coordinated with the leg motion in any desired way. It was determined solely by the relationship of the crank arms to the oval shape of the chain wheel.

The "Thetic" chain wheel of the '30s was widely used, both in racing and in general cycling. Further experimentation with oval chain wheels—some very exaggerated—has continued on and off since then. Quite a bit of academic testing has accompanied this experimentation and the research has suggested the value of the device nearly beyond question. So it is somewhat mysterious to me that the device is not generally available today. I am aware that oval chain wheels have been produced sporadically over the years—there may even be one or more on the market now—but they have lost the acceptance by the cycling public that they had at the outset. I am also aware that the concept has been attacked fairly vigorously by some in the cycling world and denounced as me-

chanical quackery. It has been suggested that the idea was spawned and fostered by ignorant people who didn't understand how to pedal a bicycle properly.

It is true, given the machinery at their disposal, that bike racers devote a lot of attention to learning to "spin" the pedals evenly and smoothly, evening out the effort—as much as possible—throughout the 360° cycle, and many fine riders have perfected this technique to a very high degree. But it must be seen, clearly, that the technique itself is merely an adaptation to necessity—a necessity imposed by the nature of the circular chain wheel. It is not an end in itself. A more efficient mechanical arrangement for transmitting force is just that. It cannot be negated or denied simply in terms of what some consider to be orthodox technique.

At any rate, oval chain wheels have come and gone, probably not receiving as much attention as they deserve. I am not aware that they are available to the interested cyclist at the present time, although they may be. An even more interesting development has appeared, however, in the work of Larry G. Brown, a Honolulu-based inventor and entrepreneur. Brown is responsible for two inventions for improving bicycle drive efficiency, both

based on the principle of the eccentric cam. A cam, by definition, is a rotary device whose contour imparts a particular motion, usually rocking or reciprocating, to a part or parts that bear against it. That's quite a mouthful. A simple example of a cam is the oval chain wheel we have just been discussing, but cams can be contoured in more precise and complicated ways in order to produce or impart a more complex or precisely defined motion. Larry Brown's cams are a far cry from ovals.

The earlier of Brown's inventions, a drive briefly marketed by Facet Enterprises under the name BioCam, is as different from the conventional drive mechanism as anything that has surfaced in the last sixty years. The BioCam drive has an eccentric cam fixed to each of the two crank arms. The cams are contoured to produce a very carefully calculated variation of pedal pressure (or, conversely, effective pedaling force) throughout the 360° pedaling arc. The circular pedaling motion is transmitted to the rear wheel hub through cam "followers," pivoted levers that bear against the cams on their lower ends and connect to longitudinal linkage rods on their upper ends. The rods, in turn, connect with short sections of standard bike chain that engage the drive sprockets on the rear hub.

In operation the rotation of the cam causes a back-and-forth motion of the followers which alternately pulls the rod–chain transmission line forward, causing the hub to rotate, and then allows it to "rewind" backward, under spring tension. The point at which the transmission rod engages the upper portion of the cam follower is variable, and the precise position determines the effective gear ratio. The system offers a greatly expanded range of gearing, compared to conventional derailleur systems: from 30 to 150 inches (!). This range is divided into some fifty ratios in small, even increments, allowing the rider to fine tune the pedal cadence very precisely.

Extensive testing was done in the early stages of BioCam development. First of all, on the practical level, two experienced American racing cyclists, Gary Holder and Alan Kingsbery, were able to break four longstanding time-trial records using the BioCam drive. Further, a number of physiological or metabolic studies were carried out investigating the question of oxygen consumption per unit work, and the effect on pulse rate of the BioCam compared to the conventional drive system. In both areas significant differences—advantages on the BioCam side—were noted. There was both a lower consumption of oxygen and a lower pulse rate with the use of the cam drive. To followers of sports medicine these are important statistics. To most, all that you really need to understand is that this means there is less fatigue for each turn of the crank. As important as any other single factor, apparently, is that the cam drive allows the muscles to work *intermittently*, in "pulses," with rest in between. This has numerous

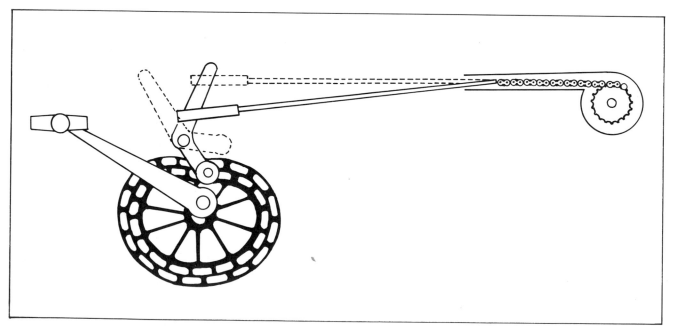

The Bio-Cam drive mechanism translates the circular pedal motion into reciprocal motion in the drive train. Working in "pulses," it gives the leg muscles a rest during each turn of the cranks.

physiological benefits. Test results suggested, in one case, that the BioCam advantage might be as high as 14 percent in overall efficiency. Other, more conservative estimates, including Brown's, put the figure at 10 to 12 percent—still a staggering improvement, considering the tiny increments that other technological innovations have been aiming at.

The BioCam bicycle is not currently available and its future is in question. Extensive litigation is likely to take place regarding the licensing of the manufacturing rights, and a fully worked out, carefully refined version of the

machine may or may not ever become a reality. Meanwhile Larry Brown has gone on to design a second cam drive for the bicycle. For all of its merit and promise the BioCam, as tested, had some drawbacks. It was not as efficient in long hill-climbing situations as a conventional drive, nor in sprint situations. In coming up with the Selectocam, Brown sought to resolve these difficulties. The solution was to combine a cam-actuated drive mechanism with a conventional, circular chain wheel and provide a shift mechanism that allows the rider to switch back and forth at will.

In the Selectocam the basic configuration of the conventional drive system is retained: chain wheel, endless chain, circular pedaling motion. What is added to this is a mechanism that, when engaged, causes the chain wheel to "float," or *move on its axis in relation to the crank arm.* In other words the cam mechanism causes the chain wheel to turn *faster* than the crank arm during part of the pedal stroke and slower at other times. The specific shape and design of the cams involved determines the precise action of the system and, by varying cam design, infinite variations are possible,

The huge oversized custom chain wheel and the extra-long derailleur cage of the Selectocam drive, designed by engineer-inventor Larry Brown.

This is the cam it- self—the mecha- nism that causes the chain wheel to revolve faster than the pedals during one phase of the cycle, slower dur- ing another phase.

suiting the needs of particular riders or riding situations.

The success of the Se- lectocam drive is attested to by the results of the 1980 running of the formidable 1,250-kilometer (750-mile) Paris–Brest–Paris race, the longest regularly held single- stage bike race anywhere. A team of five American riders—experienced racers, but definitely newcomers to the intensely competitive Eu- ropean racing scene—showed up for the race with Selecto-

cam-equipped bicycles. Amer- icans are not generally con- sidered by European bike racers to be in the same league, and the bikes, with their unusually large chain wheels (higher gears, requir- ing stronger legs), prompted some smiles. Nevertheless results speak louder than pre- conceptions or a thousand ac- ademic arguments. What the Selectocam (or any cam drive) does is allow the rider to push a higher gear than he or she would be able to without it. Despite a number of re-

lated hassles in addition to the arduousness of the race it- self, the leading member of the team, Scott Dickson, as- tounded all but Larry Brown by placing *second* in a field of 1,800 starters. Two other team members placed in the top thirty.

While Brown's cam drives have demonstrated such remarkable and promis- ing results on upright, con- ventional bicycles, they may find even more efficient appli- cation in the newly emerging breed of recumbent cycles. The recumbent position would take even more advantage of the emphasis on the push phase of the pedaling cycle, with more of the total musculature aiding the legs.

Speculative esitmates for an overall efficiency increase for a recumbent cycle equipped with a cam drive range up to 25 percent over the finest conventional bicycles. Again, considering the performance-increase increments that the cycling world has been dealing with over much of the last seventy or eighty years, changes of this magnitude place the bicycle in a different universe.

H.P.V's: THE CULMINATION OF BICYCLE TECHNOLOGY

As early as 1919 the French cyclist-inventor, Marcel Berthet, began breaking time-trial and distance records using bicycles with streamlined fairings. Berthet's activities continued into the 1930s. The first recumbent bicycle, the French Velocar, came along in 1933 and began to break every record in sight. Much more recently, in 1974, cyclist and former Olympian Ron Skarin rode an experimental streamlined bicycle designed by Dr. Chester Kyle, a professor of mechanical engineering at California State University, Long Beach. The dash was clocked at over 43 miles per hour—a new unofficial record. The word unofficial is used advisedly for, in each of these cases and many more, the *Federation Internationale Cycliste* (FIC) has refused to recognize the achivements. These machines were not bicycles. The message was clear. Users of unconventional technology need not apply—for FIC recognition anyway.

Dissatisfied with this state of affairs, Professor Kyle, and some other folks with a passionate interest in experimenting with the performance capabilities of muscle-powered machines, organized the International Human-Powered Vehicle Association to encourage research and application of new technology to transport vehicles, mostly cycles. The move was in many ways long overdue, and it is amazing to reflect on the speed of the progress that has taken place since the organization has been around to provide a focus to what were previously widely scattered and generally isolated efforts.

The most visible manifestation of the IHPVA is the annual Speed Championships, first held in 1975 at the Ontario (California) Motor Speedway. Included in the weekend-long meet were a one-hour distance trial and a moderate-length road race, both of which tested the practicality of the entrants. But most attention was, and still is, focused on the speed trials in which each entrant was given three passes through the timing "traps"—a 200-meter stretch at the end of a half-mile approach strip. The timing was only of the final 200 meters. Entries were divided into single-rider and multiple-rider categories.

The turnout was light in '75, but the results spoke loudly. The Ron Skarin–Chet Kyle association—the one that had set this whole Cecil B. DeMille scene in motion in the first place—came through to capture the Speed Championship in the single-rider category. The machine was basically a conventional bicycle with a streamlined fairing much like a vertical airplane wing. The winning pace was 44.69 mph. This time was narrowly bested for the overall speed honors by an original-design tandem vehicle, the work of Phil Norton and Chris Deeton. Their speed through the traps was 44.97 mph, a tiny margin of victory.

Anyway, the Championships were launched. The seeds were sown and innovations followed rapidly one upon another in the years that followed. One of the lessons that had been learned at the first IHPVA Speed Championships was that, while

winglike fairings provided a significant advantage in moving a cyclist through still air, they acted like sails in crosswinds, tending to knock the cyclist over sideways—a major problem.

A vehicle that went quite far in the direction of solving that problem was unveiled at the Championships the following year, 1976, by Dr. Allan Abbott. (Abbott had already traveled faster on a bicycle than any other human being past or since. He set the world motor-paced speed record of 138.67 mph in 1973, riding a bike of his own design behind a racing car.) The most salient feature of Abbott's '76 Speed-Championships entry was its low profile. It stood no more than 30 inches high. The configuration of this bicycle required the rider to pedal in a prone position, actually suspended from the top of the structure.

Dr. Abbott personally powered his own low-profile cycle to a new unassisted muscle-powered speed record of 47.8 mph, and a new era of projectile-shaped HPVs was launched.

Following his victory and the setting of the new record, Dr. Abbott retired from active participation in the Championships, at the same time performing an act that provided immense stimulus for future development by others. He decided that the

national highway speed limit of 55 mph was one that cyclists should be able to break and he established a prize for the first unassisted cycle to perform this feat. The goal, then, became clearly focused for all—there was a number to aim at. Two special conditions of the prize were a 1 mph handicap for single-rider vehicles (they could collect on hitting 54 mph) and an increase in the prize for each year it remained unclaimed.

Abbott's legacy was clearly present in the third annual Championships in 1977. The winner in the single-rider category was a low, prone-position vehicle designed by auto engineer Paul Van Valkenburgh. Its rider, Ralph Therrio, used both hands and feet for propulsion—an idea that has gained firm acceptance in more recent designs.

The winner in the multi-rider category was another low-slung, projectile-shaped vehicle named "White Lightning" by its designers, a trio of undergraduate engineering students from Northrop University, Tim Brunner, Chris Deilke, and Don Guichard. White Lightning was developed with the aid of wind-tunnel research. The shape they chose for their fairing was a fairly standard aircraft-wing profile, one that has very low drag properties. The design depended on the smoothness of the exterior surface for its low drag. The designers reportedly spent thousands of hours carefully laminating the fiberglass and plastic shell. Pedaled by cycle sprinters Jan Russell and Butch Stinton, White Lightning carried off the overall speed honors with a run of 47.4 mph. So '77 turned out to be a year in which certain design concepts were consolidated while no actual performance improvement was achieved.

The next year was a

The famous White Lightning on May 6, 1978, the day that hopes for shattering the 55 mph goal were dashed by a faulty timer. Its fastest recorded time that day—54.43 mph— was good enough to carry off 1st place honors for multi-rider vehicles—and overall. The White Lightning team returned the following year to break the 55 mph barrier on the very first try.

different matter altogether. The White Lightning team was back for a return engagement and succeeded in capturing most of the attention. On its first pass through the traps in the speed trials, the tandem broke the 50 mph barrier with ease. The second pass was timed at 53.45 mph. Psyched up to top 55 mph and carry off the prize, Russell and Stinton churned through the course a third time. Their speedometer read 56 all the way through the 200 meters, but apparent victory turned into heartbreaking anticlimax: The electronic timing equipment had failed and their time was not officially recorded. A fourth run was offered as a courtesy but, bucking slightly increased headwinds and with slightly lower spirits, they fell just short at 54.43 mph.

In the 1979 Championships, then, the prize was certain to be carried off. By general agreement the first pass was offered to White Lightning, the rest of the places being determined by lottery as usual. Russell and Stinton made short work of the element of suspense by registering 55.85 on their very first pass, eventually reaching a record 56.7 mph.

White Lightning's triumph was just the start of things, however. Before the weekend was over the first single-rider vehicle succeeded in surpassing the 55 mark. This was one in what has become a long line of Vector models produced by a team of engineers from General Dynamics, headed by Allan Voigt. This first single-rider Vector used a teardrop or fish-shaped fairing unlike the "wingtip" shape of the White Lightning. Underneath was a quite simple supine recumbent—not bicycle, but *tricycle*. The addition of the third wheel achieved a degree of lateral stability that none of the two wheel designs could hope to equal. Apparently the added weight was more than compensated for by the other design improvements.

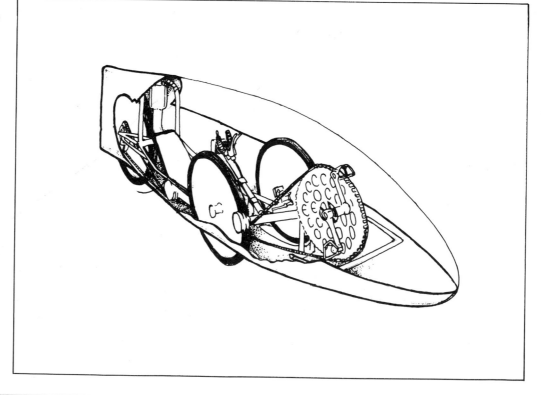

Cutaway view of the Vector 'Beta' reveals numerous unconventional features: joy-stick controls, linked front wheel steering, 100-tooth chain wheel, and low-slung recumbent seating.

Capturing the overall speed honors for the weekend was another Vector vehicle, this one a triplet, with a run of 57.07 mph.

In succeeding years other Vector designs have continued to dominate the Speed Championships. In 1980 a second-generation Vector tandem, the Gamma, achieved the fastest speed yet recorded, a blistering 62.72 mph, while an improved single-rider Vector, Beta, managed 56.55. The results of the 1981 Championships were not substantially different, either in terms of the winners or the times. In fact the fastest multi-rider time, posted by the Gamma tandem, was substantially slower than its previous year's performance.

So, again, a plateau has been reached. But it is a high plateau. In the historically brief span of six years, since the first IHPVA Speed Championships in which winning times were 50 percent faster than world-class racing speeds on conventional bikes, performance gains have been amazing. The fastest entrants have moved their vehicles at speeds approaching twice what a conventional racer can maintain. Other technical and design breakthroughs are bound to make the gap even wider. One fairly obvious line of development would be to combine the aerodynamic recumbent design with its low profile and low center of gravity with a cam drive *à la* Larry Brown. It would not be at all surprising to have such a vehicle turn up in the near future. Other innovations, the nature of which we can only guess at now, are undoubtedly taking shape in the fertile minds of dedicated inventors at this very moment.

What does all this cutting-edge technology augur for the layman? That is a subject of hot debate at the moment. The vehicles that fly down the course at Ontario Speedway are far too costly to be available to most, even if there were a provision for such vehicles on our roads and highways. Clearly many changes would have to take place, both in our economy and in the shape of our landscape, before widespread use of such cycles could become a reality. Some of the debaters are skeptics; others are visionaries. Into the latter category fits the Vector design team. They have come up with a production "commercial" version of their single-rider design, which you can try out for yourself.

Just send your check for $10,000 to Early Winters in Seattle, Washington.

The Zzipper Fairing: The Bubble that Will Not Burst

One of the more intriguing technological innovations to come to cycling in the recent past is a small, lightweight bubble of Lexan plastic: the Zzipper fairing.

Even at the modest speed of 10 miles per hour, more than half a cyclist's energy is expended fighting what is called air drag—that is, moving the air around himself and the bike. At 20 mph that proportion rises to more than three-quarters of the energy output. At racing speeds in the 30 mph range, well over 90 percent of the rider's effort goes into pushing air. It is, to say the least, a drag.

Relatively little attention has been given to this aspect of bicycle performance until recently, and certainly not on the level of the ordinary cyclist. The Zzipper is the first commercially available fairing for a conventional upright bi-

cycle to my knowledge. Its visual simplicity belies the high degree of design sophistication that has gone into the creation of the Zzipper. The fairing is a product of thorough, systematic research and testing, carried out largely in person by its designer, Glen Brown. (Brown is an aeronautical engineer out of the California Institute of Technology, and a specialist in applications of aerodynamics and fluid mechanics to problems of land transport vehicles.)

While the purpose of a fairing is to reduce air drag as much as possible, it must do so without having a deleterious effect on the handling of the bike. Brown experimented with numerous configurations, including a number of designs that offered greater "coverage" than the eventual product, but most of these introduced undesirable handling problems in crosswinds.

What the Zzipper offers the cyclist is an approximate 20 percent reduction in air drag, which translates into about a 7 percent increase in overall efficiency on level ground. In high-speed situations the fairing seems to actually improve bike stability and handling. By virtue of its shielding function the fairing also reduces windchill in cold weather.

The Zzipper is a thin shell of Lexan, a tough polycarbonate plastic that is clear and virtually shatterproof. The weight of the complete unit is well under a pound. The fairing is easily attached to (and detached from) the bicycle in a matter of seconds. It does not interfere with the operation of the brakes and its shape accommodates all standard handlebar packs. The new model, the Zzipper T, is vertically adjustable to allow for different physiques and riding positions.

The Pacer 2000 H: Solid-State Circuitry Comes to Cycling

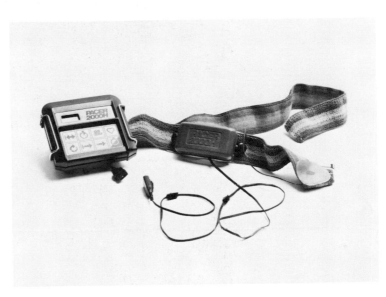

There are not many ways in which the cyclist has been directly touched by the recent leaps and bounds of electronics technology—indirectly, yes, in the form of such things as computer-assisted equipment design, but not in the form of the equipment itself. Now, at last, there is a true electronic gee-whiz gadget for the serious cyclist.

In this sense, the Pacer 2000 H is to the cyclist what the chiming, tune-playing, waterproof, liquid-crystal diode calculator-wristwatch is to the ordinary citizen. It combines "techs-appeal" with several real and serious practical purposes.

The Pacer is a small, lightweight, battery-powered multifunction sensor-calculator. The main unit mounts on the handlebars. Two magnetic sensors keep track of pedal cadence and wheel revolutions while a miniaturized sensor strapped to the rider's abdomen keeps its electronic ear on heart rate.

The Pacer is a serious training aid. It functions as a timer, as a distance calculator, and as a speedometer. It cross-calculates to give average speed over total trip time. Its most important function, however, would seem to be as a heart-rate monitor. That, at any rate, is what sets it apart from the wristwatch mentioned above. In today's methodical, scientific training regimens, awareness of the heart rate and understanding of how it relates to aerobic and anaerobic levels of work are essential.

The Pacer is already in use in many training programs, both group and individual. It has also been used as a pacing device in long, taxing endurance rides. One particular place where a number of Pacers have shown up is the annual Human-Powered Speed Championships.